What Do We Know About the Effects of Pornography After Fifty Years of Academic Research?

T0386192

This book presents an innovative cross-disciplinary report on research across the humanities and social sciences about the relationship between pornography and its consumers.

For policy makers and the wider public it can be difficult to obtain a clear understanding of the current state of knowledge on pornography and its relationships with audiences, due to the often-contradictory nature of research spanning the various and politically diverse academic disciplines. The cross-disciplinary expertise of the author team has engaged in an extensive examination of the findings of academic research in the area in order to explain, in a clear and accessible style, the most important conclusions about the relationship of pornography to Healthy Sexual Development.

This short and accessible overview is suitable for students and scholars in Psychology, Sexual Health, Film Studies, Sex Education, Queer Theory, Gender Studies, Sexuality Studies, Sociology, Media Studies and Cultural Studies.

Alan McKee is a Professor in Digital and Social Media at the University of Technology Sydney, Australia, and an expert on entertainment and healthy sexual development. He recently completed an Australian Research Council Discovery grant entitled 'Pornography's effects on audiences: explaining contradictory research data'. He also worked on an ARC Linkage grant with True (previously Family Planning Queensland) to investigate the use of vulgar comedy to reach young men with information about healthy sexual development. He has published on entertainment education for healthy sexuality in journals including the *Archives of Sexual Behavior*, the *International Journal of Sexual Health*, the *Journal of Sex Research* and *Sex Education*.

Katerina Litsou is a PhD researcher of psychology at the University of Southampton, UK. She has conducted research on pornography use and she is specifically interested in women's pornography use. She has a BSc in Psychology and an MA in Master of Sexology.

Paul Byron is a postdoctoral researcher of digital and social media at the University of Technology Sydney, Australia. He has undertaken qualitative research on young people's digital intimacies, including studies of dating/hook-up app use, pornography, sexual health and LGBTQ+ communities online. His current research focuses on LGBTQ+ young people's digital peer support for mental health. He is author of the book *Digital Media, Friendship and Cultures of Care* (Routledge 2021).

Roger Ingham is a Professor of Health and Community Psychology at the University of Southampton, UK, and Director of the Centre for Sexual Health Research. He has been conducting research into many aspects of sexual and reproductive health and related issues for over 30 years, he has published widely and has worked with governments and other local and international agencies in many countries. His undergraduate degree in Psychology was obtained from University College London, UK, and his DPhil was awarded by the University of Oxford, UK.

Focus on Global Gender and Sexuality

Reading Iraqi Women's Novels in English Translation
Iraqi Women's Stories
Ruth Abou Rached

Gender Hierarchy of Masculinity and Femininity during the Chinese Cultural Revolution
Revolutionary Opera Films
Zhuying Li

Representations of Lethal Gender-Based Violence in Italy Between Journalism and Literature
Femminicidio Narratives
Nicoletta Mandolini

LGBTQI Digital Media Activism and Counter-Hate Speech in Italy
Sara Gabai

Transmasculinity on Television
Patrice A. Oppliger

What Do We Know About the Effects of Pornography After Fifty Years of Academic Research?
Alan McKee, Katerina Litsou, Paul Byron and Roger Ingham

What Do We Know About the Effects of Pornography After Fifty Years of Academic Research?

Alan McKee, Katerina Litsou, Paul Byron and Roger Ingham

Routledge
Taylor & Francis Group

LONDON AND NEW YORK

First published 2022
by Routledge
4 Park Square, Milton Park, Abingdon, Oxon OX14 4RN

and by Routledge
605 Third Avenue, New York, NY 10158

Routledge is an imprint of the Taylor & Francis Group, an informa business

British Library Cataloguing-in-Publication Data
A catalogue record for this book is available from the British Library

Library of Congress Cataloging-in-Publication Data
A catalog record has been requested for this book

ISBN: 978-1-032-14031-5 (hbk)
ISBN: 978-1-032-14033-9 (pbk)
ISBN: 978-1-003-23203-2 (ebk)

DOI: 10.4324/9781003232032

Typeset in Times New Roman
by Deanta Global Publishing Services, Chennai, India

Contents

Acknowledgements

The authors would like to thank Ash Watson for her brilliant, efficient and friendly research assistance work on porn literacies research, reported in Chapter 6.

The research reported in this book was supported by the Australian Research Council Discovery grant DP170100808 'Pornography's effects on audiences: explaining contradictory research data'.

Alan McKee: I would like first to thank my husband, Anthony Spinaze because every time I publish a book he asks 'Is it about me?'. I would like to thank Professor John Hartley, who introduced me to the world of academic research with generosity and humour and got me excited about the possibilities of researching culture. I am deeply indebted to my co-authors on this book – for five years our meetings and emails have sparked curiosity, excitement, joy and hilarity, and have reminded me that good academic research relationships are necessarily good relationships between human beings. I remain profoundly grateful to my colleagues who have helped me over the years develop my thinking about sex and entertainment – in particular Kath Albury, Feona Attwood, Larissa Behrendt, Jerry Coleby-Williams, Catharine Lumby, John Mercer, Susanna Paasonen, Clarissa Smith, Rebecca Sullivan and Ann Watson. I would not be able to do this work without the support of the University of Technology Sydney, a great place to be a Communications researcher, where I work with outstanding colleagues. I'm particularly delighted to find myself this year appointed as a Professor of Digital and Social Media: the enthusiasm, creativity and intelligence of my new colleagues in that team inspires me. All mistakes and eccentricities that I have contributed to this book remain my own.

Paul Byron: I firstly wish to thank Alan McKee for inviting me to work on this project, all those years ago, and for mentorship beyond this project. Big thanks to Roger Ingham and Katerina Litsou for being fine collaborators and expanding my 'undisciplined' thinking on pornography research. I've learned far more than I expected from this project, and I look forward to seeing where our work travels. Thanks to the many mentors, peer researchers, academics and friends whose writings and conversations have assisted my understanding of pornography research and where it intersects with studies of digital media and health and wellbeing. There are too many to mention, but particular thanks to Kath Albury, Susanna Paasonen, Feona Attwood and Clarissa Smith. I'd also like to thank the Digital and Social Media team at UTS, and my partner Nicholas, for ongoing support when writing (or at least trying to).

Roger Ingham: I was not quite sure what to say when Alan first invited me to join him in the grant bid to the ARC – but being a great fan of his healthy sexual development work I was flattered and excited. I have never regretted the decision. He has been inspirational, hard-working, clear-headed and open-minded throughout, as have the staff on the project – Paul and Katerina. It has been a real pleasure to have been part of the team exploring this most enigmatic of topics. Many thanks to the Delphi panel members, the initial advisory group, and all the journal reviewers and editors who have read bits along the way and offered (mainly) constructive feedback.

Katerina Litsou: I would like to thank Roger Ingham, Alan McKee and Paul Byron who actually introduced me into the world of pornography research. I would like to give my special thanks to Roger Ingham for giving the opportunity to work on this project and supporting me all the way through.

The authors acknowledge that some of the material in this book has previously been published in different forms in the following sources:

Chapter 2: Litsou, K., McKee, A., Byron, P., & Ingham, R. (2020). Productive disagreement during research in interdisciplinary teams: Notes from a case study investigating pornography and healthy sexual development. *Issues in Interdisciplinary Studies, 38*(1–2), 101–125.

Chapter 3: McKee, A., Byron, P., Litsou, K., & Ingham, R. (2020). An interdisciplinary definition of pornography: Results from a global Delphi panel. *Archives of Sexual Behavior, 49*(3), 1085–1091. https://doi.org/10.1007/s10508-019-01554-4

Chapter 4: McKee, A., Litsou, K., Byron, P., & Ingham, R. (2021a). The relationship between consumption of pornography and consensual sexual practice: Results of a mixed method systematic review. *Canadian Journal of Human Sexuality, 30*(3), 387–396. https://doi.org/10.3138/cjhs.2021-0010

Chapter 5: Litsou, K., Byron, P., McKee, A., & Ingham, R. (2021). Learning from pornography: Results of a mixed methods systematic review. *Sex Education, 21*(2), 236–252. https://doi.org/10.1080/14681811.2020.1786362

Chapter 6: Byron, P., McKee, A., Watson, A., Litsou, K., & Ingham, R. (2021). Reading for realness: Porn literacies, digital media, and young people. *Sexuality & Culture, 25*(3), 786–805. https://doi.org/10.1007/s12119-020-09794-6

Chapter 7: McKee, A., Litsou, K., Byron, P., & Ingham, R. (2021b). The relationship between consumption of pornography and sexual pleasure: Results of a mixed-method systematic review. *Porn Studies, 8*(3), 331–344. https://doi.org/10.1080/23268743.2021.1891564

1 Fifty years of academic research on pornography

Alan McKee, Roger Ingham, Paul Byron and Katerina Litsou

Introduction

Why do we need to understand the relationships between pornography and people who use it?

'If you ask some people', notes the journalist Olga Khazan, 'America is in the middle of a public-health crisis':

> Legislators in 16 states have passed resolutions declaring that pornography, in its ubiquity, constitutes a public-health crisis. The wave of bills started five years ago, with Utah, which went a step further this spring by passing a law mandating that all cellphones and tablets sold in the state block access to pornography by default.
>
> (Khazan, 2021, np)

Lobbyists argue that pornography has negative effects, including that it:

> increases problematic sexual activity among teens, normalizes violence against women, contributes to sex trafficking, causes problems in intimate relationships, and is 'potentially biologically addictive.'
>
> (Khazan, 2021)

However, despite this vigorous and visible campaigning against pornography, Khazan notes that the evidence on the issue is not clear: 'Whether porn is actually harming the health of adults who watch it is frustratingly hard to determine' (Khazan, 2021, np). Despite the assertions of campaigners that pornography has straightforward effects, it is difficult to get a clear overview of what academic research tells us about the relationship between the consumption of sexually explicit materials and healthy sexual development. Where would interested researchers, politicians, journalists – and

DOI: 10.4324/9781003232032-1

even parents who might be worried about the effects of pornography on young people – go for such an account?

In 2017, the four authors of this book set out to review the academic research that has been published about this topic across academic disciplines; and then to synthesise that information and present it in a way that would be meaningful and accessible for researchers, parents, policymakers and interested others. It was a major project. It took us years to work out how we could identify relevant research, and how we could bring together the findings of researchers in different academic disciplines that might have different assumptions about how pornography research should be conducted, what questions are worth asking and what counts as evidence. It took a long time to read hundreds of articles and agree within our own team about what they were saying (and/or not saying). But, in the end, we did it. This book is the result.

Healthy sexual development

In order to start exploring the relationship between the consumption of pornography and healthy sexual development we need to answer the question:

What is healthy sexual development?

It is an important question, one that we discuss in all kinds of tangential ways every day, through news stories about sexting and casual sex, about objectification and sexual harassment and, of course, through discussions about pornography (the focus of this book). We talk about all of these kinds of culture, and the effects they have on our sex lives, positive or negative. But, strangely, we rarely talk directly about the fundamental question – what exactly is a happy, healthy sex life? We have discussions about whether sexting leads people to have more sexual partners, for example, without ever asking – is it a good thing or a bad thing if people have more sexual partners? We worry that pornography might be putting people off having physical sexual relationships – but don't ask whether that is necessarily problematic.

Sexual health is defined by the World Health Organisation as:

> a state of physical, emotional, mental and social well-being in relation to sexuality; it is not merely the absence of disease, dysfunction or infirmity. Sexual health requires a positive and respectful approach to sexuality and sexual relationships, as well as the possibility of having pleasurable and safe sexual experiences, free of coercion, discrimination and violence. For sexual health to be attained and maintained, the sexual rights of all persons must be respected, protected and fulfilled.
>
> (World Health Organisation, 2006, p. 5)

But what does that mean in day-to-day practice for those of us who might be having sex?

The first important point we want to make is that healthy sexual development isn't the same for everybody. There are many different ways in which you can have a happy, healthy sex life. You can be married in the suburbs with two kids having sex once a week with the lights off. Or you can be single, going out dancing, picking up strangers and having enthusiastic, sweaty fun in the toilets of a nightclub. You can be in a committed three-some; or an extended network of polyamorous fuckbuddies and friends-with-benefits. You can enjoy spanking or roleplaying or being wrapped in cellophane and suspended from the ceiling. A healthy sex life can involve oral sex or anal sex or vaginal sex or many other body parts. Or maybe you've decided that sex isn't really your thing and what you really want is a life of cuddling and boardgames. All of these can be examples of sexually healthy lives.

But the variation isn't infinite. Underlying all of these many different ways to be a healthy sexual being are 15 'domains' of healthy sexual development, identified in 2010 by a group of researchers across a range of academic disciplines – child psychology, early childhood, a legal expert in children's rights, a specialist in sexuality education, experts on sexual socialisation, and experts on the media's impact on children's development (McKee et al., 2010). According to these experts, healthy sexual development should meet 15 criteria:

1. *Freedom from unwanted activity*. Healthy sexual development takes place in a context in which we are protected from unwanted sexual activity. This is a fundamental starting point.
2. *Sexual development should not be aggressive, coercive or joyless*. The best sexual development is 'fun', playful and light-hearted (Okami et al., 1998, p. 364).
3. *Education about sexual practice*. We all need to have accurate knowledge about how our bodies work.
4. *Awareness of public/private boundaries*. One of the earliest things we learn about a healthy sex life that while sex itself is nothing to be ashamed about, we must make distinctions about what we perform in private and what we perform in public.
5. *An understanding of consent*. We must learn what consent is, the complexity of the consent, and its fundamental place in healthy sexual practice.
6. *An understanding of safety*. What are the risks involved in becoming a sexual being? These include not only physical risks such as unplanned pregnancy or Sexually Transmitted Infections, but a range of other risks

– the emotional risks of becoming involved in an abusive relationship; or the more mundane risk of being trapped in a boring relationship.

7. *Self-acceptance*. We need to develop a positive attitude, rather than a shameful one, towards our own sexual beings – whether that's our body shape, our sexual identities, or the sexual pleasures that we prefer.

8. *Acceptance that sex can be pleasurable*. We all need to accept that sex can be pleasurable, and that's fine. Again, it's nothing to be ashamed of. We do not need to feel guilty because we enjoy physical pleasure.

9. *Sexual agency*. If we want to communicate assertively what we want from sex and relationships, we need to know what it is that we want. To grow up as healthy, happy sexual beings we need to know that each of us has the right to the final say about what we do with our bodies, and to explore what we enjoy.

10. *Relationship skills*. We need to learn the skills that underlie all healthy human relationships; for example, how to be assertive without being aggressive in communicating what we want.

11. *Open communication*. It's difficult to have a healthy sex life if you're ashamed to talk about what you want and what you enjoy. Growing up in a supportive environment can help us communicate openly about sex; if we don't have that environment when we're younger we can work on developing these skills later in our lives.

12. *Lifelong learning*. Healthy sex lives don't stop evolving the first time we have sex. We can continue learning and developing throughout our lives.

13. *Resilience*. In sexual practice, as in many other areas of our lives, we will make mistakes. Do we have the skills to learn from these, and to grow from them?

14. *Understanding of parental and societal values*. All of these aspects of healthy sexual development occur within a cultural context and we need to be aware of that and know how to navigate it. That doesn't mean that we just accept negative values around us – such as homophobia or whorephobia. But we can't be naïve about them either.

15. *Competence in mediated sexuality*. We are surrounded by mediated messages about sex – from entertainment, education, religious groups … we need to learn how to use different kinds of media appropriately. Pornography is often designed for entertainment rather than as an instruction manual. Religious teachings about sex are often designed to maintain patriarchal control of women's and queers' bodies and are not fit-for-purpose as sex education.

In this book we explore what we know, after 50 years of academic research, about the relationship between consuming pornography and some of the key domains of healthy sexual development. We conducted a series of literature reviews that looked at the research that has been produced from a range of academic disciplines, synthesised the results, and we present them here for your interest and application.

The big bang of modern pornography research

Why does this project refer to 'fifty years of academic research'? There's a simple reason – modern academic research about pornography was born on the 1 October 1970 when the US President's Commission on Obscenity and Pornography released its *Report* (Commission on Obscenity and Pornography, 1970). Just as in cosmology's Big Bang, where all of the matter and energy currently existing in the universe was released from a singularity, so the attitudes, approaches, methods, questions and modes of public debate that still surround academic research about pornography emerged – remarkably fully formed – with the publication of this *Report*.

The Commission was formed by the US Congress in 1967 as part of the progressive 'Great Society' social program of president Lyndon Johnson (Lewis, 2008, p. 8), tasked to 'study the effect of obscenity and pornography upon the public, and particularly minors, and its relationship to crime and other antisocial behavior' (Commission on Obscenity and Pornography, 1970, p. 1), to analyse the laws controlling obscenity and pornography, to report on the volume of such material being distributed in America and to make recommendations for 'legislative, administrative, or other appropriate action' (p. 1). The President appointed the 18 members of the Commission in January 1968 and it was given two million US dollars (Hill et al., 1970, p. 458) (equivalent to almost US14 million in 2021 money) and two years to complete 'its studies' (Commission on Obscenity and Pornography, 1970, p. 1).

And the Commission did indeed take 'its studies' seriously. Starting with an 'initial survey of available information', it noted 'the insufficiency of existing factual evidence as the basis for recommendations' – and so the Commission 'initiated a program of research, designed to provide empirical information relevant to its tasks' (p. 2). We can see how seriously the Commission took its work by reviewing the material it released two years later. In addition to the *Report of the Commission on Obscenity and Pornography* – which itself runs to 700 pages – the Commission also released a separate *Technical Report* reproducing the results of all the academic research it commissioned for the process. This mammoth publication runs to a total of nine volumes, numbered in Roman numerals I–IX; a total of 2,760 pages, and 81 academic articles.

The pre-big bang world of research on the effects of pornography is summarised in the articles in Volume I of the *Technical Report*. As well as reports of pilot studies and methodological work, Volume I provides reviews of the existing academic literature at the time. In their 'evaluative review' of recent psychological research about 'sex censorship', Cairns, Paul and Wishner look for research about any 'long-term behavioral effects of exposure to "obscene" materials' (Cairns et al., 1971, p. 6). Two points are of interest here. The first is the use of the term 'exposure' to describe the relationship between audiences and pornography. This word has different implications to terms such as 'consumption' or 'use' of pornography – we discuss this, and our position on terminology, in the next chapter. Secondly, they note particular public interest in whether exposure to pornography led to the commission of sex crimes, or other kinds of crimes:

> Unfortunately there were no empirical studies of even the *immediate* or short-term behavioral effects of obscene or pornographic stimuli on the individual, much less the effects upon the standards of a society. Investigations of long-term effects were non-existent.
>
> (Cairns et al., 1971, p. 6)

Also in Volume I, Lenore Kupperstein offers 'A review of the research literature' on the 'role of pornography in the etiology of juvenile delinquency' (Kupperstein, 1971) – another common concern at the time. But, reviewing the academic literature on the causes of juvenile delinquency she finds nothing of relevance:

> exposure to and consumption of pornography are nowhere mentioned in the professional literature on the etiology of delinquency nor is there any suggestion as to their probable significance.
>
> (Kupperstein, 1971, p. 109)

Volume II of the *Technical Report* is dedicated to legal analysis by authors including the Commission's general counsel, Paul Bender. These review US legislation and case history and present comparisons with other countries. Volumes III and IV present data about 'The Marketplace' for pornography in America, including a national industry analysis authored by lawyer John Sampson; and a series of empirical case studies of particular cities and types of consumption by an economist, a lawyer, an anthropologist, a sociologist and a criminologist. Volume V – addressing 'Societal control mechanisms' – is organised around possible ways of managing sexual materials, and provides analysis of the workings of law enforcement, citizen action groups, industry self-regulation and sex education. These chapters are authored by social and clinical psychologists, legal scholars and a sociologist. Volume VI reports on the findings of a 'National Survey' designed, administered and reported on by a market research group.

Volumes VII and VIII of the *Technical Report* are most directly relevant to this project, presenting 30 articles on the effects of pornography under the headings 'Erotica and Antisocial Behavior' (VII) and 'Erotica and Social Behavior' (VIII). Many of these take a social psychological approach to ask whether 'exposure' to pornography leads people to become sexually violent or aggressive (Cook & Fosen, 1971; Goldstein et al., 1971; Johnson et al., 1971; Walker, 1971). Others take legal (Ben-Veniste, 1971; Mosher & Katz, 1971) or criminological (Kupperstein & Wilson, 1971; Kutchinsky, 1971) approaches to look at national-level correlations between the availability of pornographic material and 'registered sex crimes' (Kutchinsky, 1971). Another group of studies take a social psychological approach to explore more generally the 'effects' of pornography – including the extent to which pornography consumers became sexually stimulated by different kinds of pornography and whether it then changes the amount or kind of sex that they have (Amoroso et al., 1971; Byrne & Lamberth, 1971; Davis & Braucht, 1971b). One study explores whether exposure to pornography leads to 'deviant sexual behaviour' such as homosexuality, promiscuity or premarital sex (Davis & Braucht, 1971a).

The final Volume of the *Technical Report*, entitled 'Consumer and the Community', presents a wide-ranging series of articles from a variety of disciplinary perspectives: a group of articles explores what people consider to be obscene, drawing on survey (Wallace et al., 1971) or experimental (Katzman, 1971a, 1971b) data. Another group of articles returns to the concerns of Volumes VII and VIII, presenting data about various groups of young people's exposure to pornographic materials (Elias, 1971), and the relationships in these groups between pornography exposure and variables including amounts of masturbation, dating and academic performance (Berger et al., 1971a), friendships with members of the opposite sex and permissiveness of sexual attitudes (Berger et al., 1971b) and antisocial behaviour (Propper, 1971). In addition, in this volume a sociologist provides a 'content analysis' of 'Sex-related themes in the underground press' (Levin, 1971); while a group of anthropologists presents data about the content and audiences of romantic confession magazines (Sonenschein, 1972). The *Technical Report* concludes with an anthropological 'cross-cultural study of modesty and obscenity' (Stephens, 1971) and a sociological account of 'the consumers of pornography where it is easily available: the Swedish experience' (Zetterberg, 1971).

On the basis of this sprawling collection of academic studies, the Commission came to the conclusion that:

> there is a correlation between experience with erotic materials and general attitudes about sex: Those who have more tolerant or liberal sexual attitudes tend also to have greater experience with sexual material.
>
> (Commission on Obscenity and Pornography, 1970, p. 30)

It also found, in relation to its task to determine the relationship between the consumption of pornography and criminality, that:

> Delinquent and nondelinquent youth generally report similar experiences with explicit sexual materials ... Available research indicates that sex offenders have had less adolescent experiences with erotica than other adults ... empirical research designed to clarify the question has found no evidence to date that exposure to explicit sexual materials plays a significant role in the causation of delinquent or criminal behavior.
>
> (Commission on Obscenity and Pornography, 1970,
> pp. 30, 31, 32)

On this basis, the Commission's recommendations included 'that a massive sex education effort be launched' (Commission on Obscenity and Pornography, 1970, p. 54), 'that federal, state and local legislation prohibiting the sale, exhibition or distribution of sexual materials to consenting adults should be repealed' (Commission on Obscenity and Pornography, 1970, p. 57), with the caveats the legislation should prohibit the sale of explicit material to 'young persons' (Commission on Obscenity and Pornography, 1970, p. 62), and 'public display' of such material (Commission on Obscenity and Pornography, 1970, p. 67).

The last 50 years of academic research on pornography consumption

Reviewing the *Report* and the *Technical Report* of the Commission at a distance of 50 years we can see the ways in which this work changed the study of pornography in Western countries and set the stage for what was to come – as well as some ways in which the innovations of the Commission have fizzled out in succeeding research.

Perhaps the most important contribution of the work of the panel was to 'place the dimension of human sexual behaviour on the agenda for continuing inquiry' (Johnson et al., 1970, p. 171). The Commission clearly promoted the idea that we needed academic research about the role of pornography in society. There exist few academic articles before 1970 that study the relationship between pornography and its audiences; in the years that followed thousands have been published. Partly this change is to do with the general increase in academic research; the academy has grown massively since the late 1960s and there are simply a lot more academics doing a lot more research. But it also represents a clear pivot away from a previous approach to pornography in which research was unimportant, Christian values were to be upheld regardless of data, and it was the voices of powerful public men (sic) that provided the context for setting policy about sexually explicit materials. We can see how revolutionary this move was at the time by looking at responses to the Commission's *Report*.

The *Report*, after its initial publication by the US Government Printing Office, was commercially published in the same year by Bantam Books, 'set in type from the materials released by the Commission to the Press on September 30 1970', with the cover blaring 'The complete text of the report now exploding into a bitter, nation-wide controversy' (Commission on Obscenity and Pornography, 1970). The Commission consisted of 18 members, as well as support and professional staff. The Commission *Report*, as well as the main 'Report', also includes two adversarial 'Reports' authored by three Commission members which radically disagree with the main *Report* (one of whom is Charles H Keating, founder of Citizens for Decent Literature and producer of the film *Perversion for Profit* (Keating, 1965)). Both of these minority Reports make clear that their disagreement with the main *Report* is the lack of attention to 'the Judeo-Christian values from which our culture and heritage is derived' (Hill et al., 1970, p. 464), and that the *Report* 'advocates sex education without reference to morality, God, or religion' (Keating Jr, 1970, p. 619):

> For those who believe in God, in his absolute supremacy as the Creator and Lawgiver or life, in the dignity and destiny which He has conferred upon the human person, in the moral code that governs sexual activity – for those who believe in such 'things', no argument against pornography should be necessary.
>
> (Keating Jr, 1970, p. 582)

From this religious viewpoint the minority Reports then go on to attack 'the scanty and manipulated evidence contained within this report', the research methods used (Hill et al., 1970, p. 463), the 'persons of mediocre talent, hangers-on in government, or individuals not yet settled on a course in life who accept interim work' who staffed the Commission (Keating Jr, 1970,

p. 582), the 'tyranny of the Commission Chairman, and the runaway Staff' (Keating Jr, 1970, p. 595).

The dissenting reports are also vexed that the Commission chose not to hold public hearings. Public hearings had previously been an accepted way of generating data to guide policy – for example, Kupperstein notes in her review of the literature on pornography and juvenile delinquency that:

> After a series of hearings in 1955, the chairman of the United States Senate Subcommittee to Investigate Juvenile Delinquency concluded that 'undoubtedly, pornography is one of the contributing factors to the increase in juvenile delinquency and sex crimes in the United States' ... This conclusion was based on extensive testimony by attorneys, police officers, customs and postal service officials, psychiatrists, school authorities, youth workers and clergymen.
>
> (Kupperstein, 1971, p. 103)

The Commission on Obscenity and Pornography had explicitly rejected the suggestion that it should hold such hearings because 'in the first stage of its work public hearings would not be a likely source of accurate data' (Commission on Obscenity and Pornography, 1970, p. 3). The dissenting Commission members were so appalled that the 'Commission under its leadership had consistently refused to go to the *public* and hear other views' (Hill et al., 1970, p. 462, emphasis in original) that they set up their own public hearings. Keating's minority Report shows the kinds of data that can be gathered in such a way: it includes in its 'Exhibit C' a range of testimonies from public luminaries:

> J Edgar Hoover: 'The circulation of periodicals containing salacious material ... play an important part in the development of crime among your youth.'
>
> (Keating Jr, 1970, p. 636)

> Herbert W Case, former Detroit Police Inspector: 'There has not been a sex murder in the history of our department in which the killer was not an avid reader of lewd magazines.'
>
> (Keating Jr, 1970, p. 637)

> Police Chief Paul E Blubaum, Phoenix, Arizona: 'Our city has experienced many crimes of sexual deviation, such as child molestation and indecent exposure. We find that most of the deviates read obscene material.'
>
> (Keating Jr, 1970, p. 637)

Keating's minority Report also provides details of pages of crimes which police attribute to the consumption of pornography. It submits a newspaper article by psychoanalyst Dr Natalie Shainess which warns that:

> pornography washes over us all like a great wave of sewage. It corrupts the body and numbs the mind ... From my own professional practice I know that the more we are exposed to things that are degrading, the more we are degraded.
>
> (Keating Jr, 1970, p. 660)

Keating further presents a speech by Robert Clegg, Headmaster of Barden Primary School in Burnley England, warning that 'sex education programmes ... amount to a deliberate attempt to interfere with ... the beliefs, standards and practices of what I would call normal people' (Keating Jr, 1970, p. 667).

This is the kind of data that had previously informed public debate about pornography – strongly held, religiously informed moral positions from people holding powerful positions in society. Against this background it is significant that the Commission refused to hold public hearings and instead insisted that 'Discussions of obscenity and pornography in the past have often been devoid of fact' and that 'Within the limits of its time and resources, the Commission has sought ... through research to broaden the factual basis for future continued discussion' (Commission on Obscenity and Pornography, 1970, p. 4).

The move towards academic research as an important source of information about the relationships between pornography and its audiences was one way in which the Commission's *Report* represented a turning point in this area. Another is that the Commission's work established that the most important questions for research in this area concern the relationship between pornography consumption and aspects of sexual behaviour – including what the Commission calls 'Social behavior' (how much, and what kinds of sex people have and their attitudes towards sex) and what they call 'Antisocial behavior' (including 'sex crimes'). Again, from our present-day vantage point this might not seem revolutionary – but at the time it was. In 1973, W Cody Wilson, the Executive Director and Director of Research for the Commission, wrote in an article on 'Pornography: the emergence of a social issue and the beginning of psychological study' for the *Journal of Social Issues* that before the Commission's work '[n]early everything imaginable has been attributed to the effects of pornography' – including not only 'sexually aggressive acts of a criminal nature' but also:

> moral breakdown, homicide, suicide, delinquency, criminal acts, indecent personal habits, unhealthy habits, unhealthy thoughts, rejection of reality, ennui [and] submission to authoritarianism.
>
> (Wilson, 1973, p. 12)

Over the intervening years, while we have seen the emergence of a well-populated literature exploring relationships between consumption of pornography and various 'social' and 'antisocial' sexual behaviours, there has been little subsequent research on whether consuming pornography turns people into (non-sex-related) murderers or criminals or leads them to submit to authoritarianism. As noted above, Kupperstein's review of the literature on the relationship between the consumption of pornography and juvenile delinquency led her to write that, as well as finding that there is no academic literature on this topic:

> nor is there any suggestion as to their probable significance, nor is there any recommendation in this literature that the relationship between pornography and delinquency merits special investigation in the future.
>
> (Kupperstein, 1971, p. 109)

The general sense that pornography can be blamed for all non-sexual ills in society does not survive as a focus of academic research after the *Report* of the Commission. The focus has been more squarely on the sexual arena.

It is also worth noting that there are some ways in which the Commission's *Report* is atypical of the research that would follow. For example, as noted above, the Commission is quite open-minded about both positive ('social') and negative ('antisocial') aspects of pornography consumption. As we will show in this book, much of the research that followed started from the assumption that the 'antisocial' effects were of greater significance and needed to be addressed.

Assessing pornography research across disciplines

In 1970, the *Report of the Commission on Obscenity and Pornography* was the big bang of modern pornography research. Fifty years later, we set out to review how our academic understanding of pornography's relationship with its audiences has changed since that founding moment. Tens of thousands of studies have been published, so what do we now know about this topic? Importantly, we wanted to gather data that have been published across the social sciences and humanities disciplines – in history, cultural studies, sociology, anthropology, social psychology and elsewhere. In one way the Commission's work was both typical and atypical of what would follow. As well as including a strong focus on social psychological research seeking to measure 'effects' of pornography consumption, the Commission also included an impressive array of different academic perspectives. As noted above, these included criminologists looking at national patterns of crime data, sociological accounts of 'Sex-related themes in the underground press' and an anthropological 'cross-cultural study of modesty and obscenity' (Stephens, 1971). As we will show in this book, our research suggests that social psychology has become perhaps the most dominant academic discipline for studying the relationships between pornography and its audiences; nevertheless, research has continued in other disciplines. Perhaps it is true that other disciplines have focused on questions other than the effects of pornography – such as research in film studies on the aesthetics of pornography; for example (Williams, 1989). It is difficult for researchers in different disciplines to understand each other's work, as we explain in the next chapter. But it is important to pay attention to, and attempt to synthesise, the data that have been gathered across academic disciplines – just as the Commission did. This has not often been done in the past 50 years. This is one of the reasons that we hope that this book will offer a unique resource for interested researchers, policymakers and public figures who want to understand what we have learned about the relationships between pornography and its audiences over the last 50 years of academic research.

Pornography research in the real world

Before we begin, it is worth noting one final way in which the Commission's *Report* set the paradigm for the pornography research that followed: it showed that pornography research would be controversial, that public debates about it would be vicious, that the participants would talk across each other, with those interested in academic research failing to communicate to those driven by religious faith and vice versa – and that some/many politicians would often favour the latter over the former. As noted above, the dissenting Reports of the Commission, speaking from the 'Judeo-Christian' point of view, violently rejected the Commission's findings. They made vicious personal attacks on the Commission members and academics with whom they disagreed. They went further: academic research and facts were, they argued, irrelevant in God's view:

> One can consult all the experts he chooses, can write reports, make studies, etc, but the fact that obscenity corrupts lies within the common sense, the reason, and the logic of every man. St Paul, looking upon a society in his time such as ours is becoming today wrote: They had exchanged God's truth for lie [sic].
>
> (Keating Jr, 1970, p. 616)

As Rainwater notes 'it is perhaps not surprising to learn that from the White House to Congress the reaction of traditional politicians to the Commission findings was hardly positive' (Rainwater, 1974, p. 143). On 2 October 1970

'Democratic and Republican leaders of the Senate expressed strong opposition … to the findings of the Commission' (Anon, 1970). The *Report* had been commissioned by Democratic President Lyndon Johnson. By the time the *Report* was delivered, Republican Richard Nixon had taken over. His public statement about the Commission's recommendations is stark:

> Several weeks ago, the National Commission on Obscenity and Pornography –appointed in a previous administration – presented its findings. I have evaluated that report and categorically reject its morally bankrupt conclusions and major recommendations. So long as I am in the White House, there will be no relaxation of the national effort to control and eliminate smut from our national life.
>
> (Nixon, 1970)

Nixon makes no attempt to engage with the academic research presented by the Commission. It is irrelevant for him – what is important is morality:

> American morality is not to be trifled with. The Commission on Pornography and Obscenity has performed a disservice, and I totally reject its report.
>
> (Nixon, 1970)

Again, this has set the template for future research on pornography: academic research does not, on the whole, guide public policy or political debate in this area. Nevertheless, we must not lose heart. We must continue to gather the evidence and make it available to stakeholders. That is the purpose of this book. In the next chapter we explain how we started the process by finding ways to examine and report on research across a range of quite different academic disciplines.

References

Amoroso, D. M., Brown, M., Pruesse, M., Ware, E. E., & Pilkey, D. W. (1971). An investigation of behavioral, psychological and physiological reactions to pornographic stimuli. In *President's Commission on Obscenity and Pornography, Technical Report* (Vol. 8, pp. 1–40). US Government Printing Office.

Anon. (1970, October 2). Senate leaders in both parties denounce findings of pornography panel. *The New York Times*. https://www.nytimes.com/1970/10/02/archives/senate-leaders-in-both-parties-denounce-findings-of-pornography.html

Ben-Veniste, R. (1971). Pornography and sex crime: The Danish experience. In *President's Commission on Obscenity and Pornography, Technical Report* (Vol. 7, pp. 245–261). US Government Printing Office.

Berger, A. S., Gagnon, J. H., & Simon, W. (1971a). Pornography: High school and college years. In *President's Commission on Obscenity and Pornography, Technical Report* (Vol. 9, pp. 165–208). US Government Printing Office.

Berger, A. S., Gagnon, J. H., & Simon, W. (1971b). Urban working-class adolescents and sexually explicit media. In *President's Commission on Obscenity and Pornography, Technical Report* (Vol. 9, pp. 209–272). US Government Printing Office.

Byrne, D., & Lamberth, J. (1971). The effect of erotic stimuli on sex arousal, evaluative responses and subsequent behavior. In *President's Commission on Obscenity and Pornography, Technical Report* (Vol. 8, pp. 41–67). US Government Printing Office.

Cairns, R. B., Paul, J. C. N., & Wishner, J. (1971). Psychological assumptions in sex censorship. In *President's Commission on Obscenity and Pornography, Technical Report* (Vol. 1, pp. 5–21). US Government Printing Office.

Commission on Obscenity and Pornography. (1970). *The report of the commission on obscenity and pornography. Special introduction by Clive Barnes of the New York Times.* Bantam Books.

Cook, R. F., & Fosen, R. H. (1971). Pornography and the sex offender - patterns of exposure and immediate arousal effects of pornographic stimuli. In *President's Commission on Obscenity and Pornography, Technical Report* (Vol. 7, pp. 149–162). US Government Printing Office.

Davis, K. E., & Braucht, G. N. (1971a). Exposure to pornography, character and sexual deviance. In *President's Commission on Obscenity and Pornography, Technical Report* (Vol. 7, pp. 173–243). US Government Printing Office.

Davis, K. E., & Braucht, G. N. (1971b). Reactions to viewing films of erotically realistic heterosexual behavior. In *President's Commission on Obscenity and Pornography, Technical Report* (Vol. 8, pp. 68–96). US Government Printing Office.

Elias, J. (1971). Exposure of adolescents to erotic materials. In *President's Commission on Obscenity and Pornography, Technical Report* (Vol. 9, pp. 273–312). US Government Printing Office.

Goldstein, M. J., Kant, H. S., Judd, L. L., Rice, C. J., & Green, R. (1971). Exposure to pornography and sexual behavior in deviant and normal groups. In *President's Commission on Obscenity and Pornography, Technical Report* (Vol. 7, pp. 1–89). US Government Printing Office.

Hill, M. A., Link, W. C., & Keating Jr, C. H. C. (1970). Report of commissioners Morton A Hill S J and Winfrey C Link, concurred in by Charles H Keating Jr. In *The report of the commission on obscenity and pornography* (pp. 456–578). Bantam Books.

Johnson, W. T., Kupperstein, L. R., & Peters, J. J. (1971). Sex offenders' experience with erotica. In *President's Commission on Obscenity and Pornography, Technical Report* (Vol. 7, pp. 163–171). US Government Printing Office.

Johnson, W. T., Kupperstein, L. R., Wilson, C. W., Larsen, O. N., Jones, G. W., Klapper, J. T., Lipton, M. A., Wolfgang, M. E., & Lockhart, W. B. (1970). The impact of erotica: Report of the effects panel to the committee on obscenity and pornography. In *President's Commission on Obscenity and Pornography,*

The Report of the Commission on Obscenity and Pornography (pp. 169–309). Bantam Books.

Katzman, M. (1971a). Photographic characteristics influencing the judgment of obscenity. In *President's Commission on Obscenity and Pornography, Technical Report* (Vol. 9, pp. 9–26). US Government Printing Office.

Katzman, M. (1971b). Relationship of socioeconomic background to judgments of sexual orientation. In *President's Commission on Obscenity and Pornography, Technical Report* (Vol. 9, pp. 1–8). US Government Printing Office.

Keating, C. (1965). *Perversion for profit*. Citizens for Decent Literature Inc. http://www.youtube.com/watch?v=zgxEh-F_Cf8

Keating Jr, C. H. (1970). Report of the commissioner Charles H Keating Jr. In *President's Commission on Obscenity and Pornography, Report of the Commissioner Charles H. Keating Jr* (pp. 578–700). Bantam Books.

Khazan, O. (2021). The porn crisis that isn't. *The Atlantic*. https://www.theatlantic.com/politics/archive/2021/06/can-you-be-addicted-porn/619040/

Kupperstein, L. (1971). The role of pornography in the etiology of juvenile deliquency. In *President's Commission on Obscenity and Pornography, Technical Report* (Vol. 1, pp. 103–111). US Government Printing Office.

Kupperstein, L., & Wilson, W. C. (1971). Erotica and antisocial behavior: An analysis of selected social indicator statistics. In *President's Commission on Obscenity and Pornography, Technical Report* (Vol. 7, pp. 311–323). US Government Printing Office.

Kutchinsky, B. (1971). Towards an explanation of the decrease in registered sex crimes in Copenhagen. In *President's Commission on Obscenity and Pornography, Technical Report* (Vol. 7, pp. 263–310). US Government Printing Office.

Levin, J. (1971). Sex-related themes in the underground press: A content analysis. In *President's Commission on Obscenity and Pornography, Technical Report* (Vol. 9, pp. 89–98). US Government Printing Office.

Lewis, J. (2008). Presumed effects of erotica: Some notes on the report of the commission on obscenity and pornography. *Film International*, *6*(6), 7–16. https://doi.org/10.1386/fiin.6.6.7

McKee, A., Albury, K., Dunne, M., Grieshaber, S., Hartley, J., Lumby, C., & Mathews, B. (2010). Healthy sexual development: A multidisciplinary framework for research. *International Journal of Sexual Health*, *22*(1), 14–19. https://doi.org/10.1080/19317610903393043

Mosher, D. L., & Katz, H. (1971). Pornographic films, male verbal aggression against women, and guilt. In *President's Commission on Obscenity and Pornography, Technical Report* (Vol. 8, pp. 357–379). US Government Printing Office.

Nixon, R. (1970). *Statement about the report of the commission on obscenity and pornography*. https://www.presidency.ucsb.edu/documents/statement-about-the-report-the-commission-obscenity-and-pornography

Okami, P., Olmstead, R., Abramson, P. R., & Pendleton, L. (1998). Early childhood exposure to parental nudity and scenes of parental sexuality ("primal scenes"): An 18-year longitudinal study of outcome. *Archives of Sexual Behavior*, *27*(4), 361–384. https://doi.org/10.1023/a:1018736109563

Propper, M. M. (1971). Exposure to sexually oriented materials among young male prisoners. In *President's Commission on Obscenity and Pornography, Technical Report* (Vol. 9, pp. 313–404). US Government Printing Office.

Rainwater, L. (1974). Editorial introduction to 'the effects of pornography'. In L. Rainwater (Ed.), *Social problems and public policy: Deviance and liberty* (p. 143). Aldine Publishing Company.

Sonenschein, D. (1972). Dynamics in the uses of erotica. *Adolescence, 7*(26), 233–244.

Stephens, W. N. (1971). A cross-cultural study of modesty and obscenity. In *President's Commission on Obscenity and Pornography, Technical Report* (Vol. 9, pp. 405–452). US Government Printing Office.

Walker, E. (1971). Erotic stimuli and the aggressive sexual offender. In *President's Commission on Obscenity and Pornography, Technical Report* (Vol. 7, pp. 91–148). US Government Printing Office.

Wallace, D., Wehmer, G., & Podany, E. (1971). Contemporary community standards of visual erotica. In *President's Commission on Obscenity and Pornography, Technical Report* (Vol. 9, pp. 27–88). US Government Printing Office.

Williams, L. (1989). *Hard core: Power, pleasure and the 'frenzy of the visible'.* University of California Press.

Wilson, C. W. (1973). Pornography: The emergence of a social issue and the beginning of psychological study. *Journal of Social Issues, 29*(3), 7–17.

World Health Organization. (2006). *Defining sexual health: Report of a technical consultation on sexual health, 28–31 January 2002.* WHO, Geneva.

Zetterberg, H. L. (1971). The consumers of pornography where it is easily available: The Swedish experience. In *President's Commission on Obscenity and Pornography, Technical Report* (Vol. 9, pp. 453–468). US Government Printing Office.

2 Method and approach[1]

Alan McKee, Paul Byron, Katerina Litsou and Roger Ingham

Designing the project

In this chapter we provide details about the research methods we used for gathering, analysing and reporting our data. This chapter is more likely to be of interest to academic readers than to other interested stakeholders – so please feel free to skip it if a discussion of the difference between correlation and causality doesn't catch your eye. If however you're concerned about epistemology, and how we justify the findings in this project, it will be of interest.

The most important thing to emphasise about the design of this project is that the authors come from a range of disciplinary backgrounds. Indeed, one of the starting points for our research was our awareness that different academic disciplines have produced very different – and sometimes even contradictory – bodies of knowledge about pornography and healthy sexual development. We wanted to understand why this is the case (McKee & Ingham, 2018). We quickly discovered that because of our variety of disciplinary backgrounds our team disagreed about many aspects of academic research. The project was designed by professors Alan McKee and Roger Ingham, two senior researchers who have practised interdisciplinary research over the course of their careers. McKee was originally trained in literary studies and media studies, the latter of which is a portmanteau area of study, including psychoanalysis, economics, social psychology and art history. He has identified as belonging to media studies and cultural studies, but over the course of his career he has led multiple interdisciplinary research projects, often seeking to establish definitional clarity across disciplines. He has co-authored research outputs with researchers from law, education, early childhood development, psychology, marketing, public health, gender studies, sociology and queer studies among other disciplines. Ingham has been researching many aspects of sexual activity amongst young people for many years, starting in the early days of HIV. He led (with

DOI: 10.4324/9781003232032-2

Peter Aggleton and John Cleland) a large DFID-funded programme on HIV in poorer countries, has worked as a consultant for the WHO and other international agencies, was research adviser for the UK government's teen-age pregnancy strategy, and has worked with other governments on various aspects of sexual health. He trained initially as a social psychologist but dips in and out of other disciplines if necessary.

McKee and Ingham then recruited two emerging researchers to work on the project. Paul Byron majored in sociology and gender studies for his undergraduate degree, worked as a health promotion officer while under-taking Honours in gender studies, and started his PhD in a social health research centre, but eventually moved to a media research centre, which later merged with an Arts and Media school. Throughout his education and research his work has mostly orbited around media and cultural studies, with a strong focus on health, gender and sexuality. He describes himself as cynical about research more committed to disciplinary principles than to social and health improvements. Katerina Litsou's work on this project is her first experience practising interdisciplinary research. She is trained as a psychologist and as a sexologist, and she identifies as a sexual health researcher, having a social science perspective on conducting research.

Despite the sometimes fractious relationship between the disciplines involved in this project, the relationship between the members of our team has been friendly and entertaining. Over the four years that we worked together we encountered and discussed a variety of disciplinary differ-ences in our approaches to pornography and healthy sexual development. Previous researchers on interdisciplinarity have made the point that, when working together in such teams, 'it's all about relationships' (Nair et al., 2008, p. 4). A project's success will depend as much on the attitudes of the team members involved as on their expertise (McNeill et al., 2001, p. 31). Although we worked very hard over the four years, and had a lot of difficult discussions, we also had fun. We laughed a lot at the differences between us, and our bemusement at those differences (you can find a lot more detail about the things we laughed about in Litsou et al., 2020). In the following chapters we provide details of what we discovered from this four-year pro-ject of reading, arguing and laughing.

The research undertaken for this book

Our starting point for this project was to put together a team of leading pornography researchers from a range of academic disciplines – what's known as a 'Delphi panel'. We began by recruiting a small Advisory Group comprising six leading professors from a range of disciplines across the Social Sciences and Humanities, selected for their expertise in healthy sexual development and/or representations of sexuality. These included researchers in Paediatrics, Epidemiology, Adolescent Medicine, Psychology, Cultural Studies and Feminist Media Studies.[2] Members of the group were asked to provide names of 'key pornography researchers around the world' to form a Delphi panel. Fifty-seven researchers were suggested by at least one of the Group members. We then contacted each of these 57 and invited them to take part. Forty-nine responded, with 40 ultimately contributing to the panel (although not every member contributed to every stage of the project). The panel included researchers from a wide range of disciplines across the humanities and social sciences, including psychology, communication studies, cultural studies, media studies, human geography, history, literary studies, film studies, gender studies, cultural anthropology, sociology and public health.[3] We asked this panel to help us define pornography, to decide what were the most important aspects of healthy sexual development in relation to pornography consumption, where we should look for relevant academic research about these relationships and what search terms we should use.

We surveyed the experts and asked the following question for each of the 15 domains of healthy sexual development (see Chapter 1) 'How important do you think this domain is in understanding the relationship between pornography and its audiences/users/consumers, etc?' Members responded on a five-point (Likert) scale from 'Very Important' to 'Completely Unimportant'. They were also asked to suggest which academic literature databases we should search, and which search terms we should use.

The members of the Delphi panel agreed that all 15 domains of HSD were 'very' or 'somewhat' important for researchers interested in understanding uses of pornography. In terms of importance, they ranked them in the following order:[4]

1. Competence in mediated sexuality
2. Awareness and acceptance that sex can be pleasurable
3. Open communication
4. Self-acceptance
5. An understanding of consent
6. Sexual agency
7. An understanding of safety
8. Lifelong learning
9. Education about sexual practice
10. Public/private boundaries
11. Understanding of parental and social values
12. Relationship skills
13. Sexual development should not be coercive or joyless

14. Freedom from unwanted activity
15. Resilience

Based on their advice we then conducted a series of systematic literature reviews of academic research on the relationship between the consumption of pornography and some of the domains of healthy sexual development. A 'systematic' literature review is one that follows an explicit and standard process that can be reproduced by future researchers, ensuring that the findings can be checked by other people to make sure that they are reasonable and do not misrepresent the data (Ressing et al., 2009, p. 457). There is also another possible approach to analysing large amounts of academic data – a 'meta-analysis', which we chose not to use. A meta-analysis only really works when there are a lot of articles taking a quantitative approach to measuring similar variables – these numbers can then be brought together and have statistical processes run on them. We chose to undertake a systematic literature review rather than a formal meta-analysis as there does not yet exist a stable and consistent set of questions, definitions and processes for data-gathering about the relationships between the consumption of pornography and healthy sexual development domains that would allow direct comparison across studies. In short, it is hard to do a meta-analysis on data that could include historical analysis of archive documents, focus group discussions with feminist researchers and varied forms of social psychological survey data. As Richters argues, it is only possible to conduct a formal meta-analysis in an area where researchers 'more or less agree about the meaning of the terms they use' (1997, p. 214) and, as Attwood and Smith have warned, we must be wary of the unproven idea that:

> research instigated and undertaken for varying purposes and within disparate academic disciplines can be aggregated to produce similar and substantiating conclusions.
>
> (Attwood & Smith, 2010, p. 175)

Rather, a process such as a systematic review that is sensitive to the ways in which different academic disciplines produce and report on data is vital when working across a range of disciplines that are not typically brought into conversation with each other. We followed the Preferred Reporting Items for Systematic Reviews and Meta-Analyses (PRISMA) guidelines (PRISMA, 2015). We started the project in 2017, and we decided to focus on research published from the period January 2000 to December 2017 rather than trying to review everything that had been published in the 50 years since the Commission's big bang. Because academic research should be cumulative, and researchers are necessarily aware of the work that has gone before them, we note that previous academic findings continue to be part of contemporary pornography research.

On the advice of the Delphi panel members, we searched four academic databases: ProQuest, EBSCO, Scopus and JSTOR. Each of these databases was nominated more than once, along with Google Scholar, but we did not use this because it does not permit searching for keywords in article abstracts.

We developed a rigorous, replicable process for conducting the reviews – this 'Search and Analysis Protocol' is available to anybody who would like to replicate our searches (http://bit.ly/3l6JvTi). The protocol is 19 pages, and almost 3,500 words long. It provides instructions about which data-bases to search, what search terms to use and how to review the articles once they have been downloaded. It provides details about exclusion criteria and intercoder reliability.[5] It provides enough information that, if a future group of researchers followed the same process, they should end up with a group of academic articles very similar to the group that we analysed.

We searched for all relevant peer-reviewed journal articles published between January 2000 and December 2017 using – for each domain – a set of search terms developed in consultation with the Delphi panel. We provide details of the search terms for each domain in the appropriate chapter. A search log template was created for inputting the search terms to ensure consistency in approach. Two members of the research team independently searched the four databases. The two members of the research team who performed the database searches each created a list containing all the articles that emerged from their searches. After removing all duplicates, lists were compared to ensure consistency. The abstract of each article was then independently reviewed in order to identify which ones were relevant to the study, using the following exclusion criteria:

- was not a peer-reviewed article;
- did not offer original qualitative or quantitative data about the consumption of pornography and the relevant domain of HSD;
- did offer original qualitative or quantitative data but in relation to another domain of healthy sexual development and not the one in focus;
- the full article was not in English;
- the article was not centrally about pornography consumption and the relevant domain of healthy sexual development.

The two coding researchers liaised closely during this process. For cases in which agreement could not be reached they brought the discussion to the whole group for a decision. This produced a final list of articles that addressed the relationship between the consumption of pornography and the relevant domain.

Two forms of analysis were then used; a light touch quantitative content analysis and a qualitative thematic analysis (Braun & Clarke, 2006). In order to facilitate the former, a spreadsheet was created to allow coding of information about research design, methods and the content of the articles. Articles were coded into this spreadsheet independently by two members of the research team using the Search and Analysis Protocol. In order to check for interrater reliability, coding was conducted in batches of ten to 15 articles and then Cohen's kappa statistic[6] was calculated for each researcher's results for each batch. If kappa was below 0.61, and as recommended by McHugh (2012), the researchers then reviewed and discussed differences, reached agreement on the coding, and then continued with the next batch of articles. This process continued until a kappa of at least 0.61 was reached for all criteria that would be coded in the analysis. For categories where it was not possible to reach a kappa of 0.61, these codes were excluded on the basis that they appeared to be too subjective (again, the full details of this process are available in the Search and Analysis Protocol).

Upon deciding which categories should be eliminated and having reached over 0.61 agreement for each remaining category, the researchers independently proceeded to code all of the remaining articles for this domain. Two members of the research team then independently carried out a thematic analysis using NVivo to identify the patterns within the research related to pornography and this particular domain of healthy sexual development. Researchers independently read the articles, using an inductive approach to identify the key 'themes' in each domain (Braun & Clarke, 2006, p. 83), with the coding sheet allowing researchers to easily identify relevant articles for analysis. The full team of researchers then discussed the possible themes identified and, over the course of several discussions, agreement was reached about the most important themes. Because the team was interdisciplinary, particular attention was paid to the differences between the ways in which articles from social sciences and humanities disciplines engaged with the themes. This generated some of the discussion of interdisciplinary research throughout the project (Litsou et al., 2020).

Another important aspect of our protocol is that because we only searched for articles that provided information about the effects of pornography consumption on healthy sexual development, we excluded a *lot* of academic research from this study. There have been thousands of articles published about the effects of pornography; however, we quickly found that the vast majority of these are not about aspects of healthy sexual development. For example, there exists a significant tradition of research about whether pornography consumption is correlated with the stability of monogamous committed relationships. Although this topic may be of interest to the researchers conducting the work, relationship stability isn't related to healthy sexual development. People can be in long-term, committed stable relationships and have terrible sex lives – and indeed, terrible relationships (staying together for 40 years doesn't mean that relationship is actually good …). Or equally, people can have wonderful sex lives without being in a relationship. So, we were surprised to find out that, for some domains of healthy sexual development, there were fewer than a dozen published articles that were relevant to the effects of pornography, out of the thousands that have been published. We will keep returning to this issue throughout the book. What have we learned from 50 years of research into the effects of pornography? Well, one thing we have learned for certain – in many cases, we've been researching the wrong things.

Another point that quickly became apparent is that, even with a team of four people working for a number of years, we would not be able to conduct systematic reviews of all 15 domains of healthy sexual development. The interdisciplinary discussions of our data became part of the project itself and meant that we didn't reach a point where the project ran like a machine. Every stage in the process for every domain involved extensive discussions between the four team members as we reviewed the data that we had produced, the interpretations we should make of it and whether we agreed on what we should count as 'data' or an 'interpretation' (for an extended discussion of these challenges, see Litsou et al., 2020). We therefore had to choose which domains of healthy sexual development we would focus on. The fact that our Delphi panel had ranked all 15 domains as being important gave us latitude in choosing the ones to focus on, but was not terribly helpful in actually making those decisions. We were able to conduct systematic reviews of four domains in the time available. In choosing the domains, we took into account both the rankings given by the expert panel, and our awareness of which issues are currently of particular interest in public discussions about pornography (as research impact and engaging with real world concerns is increasingly important for academic researchers). On this basis, we chose to review 'Competence in mediated sexuality' – that is, media/porn literacy – which was ranked number one by our Delphi panel, and has become an increasingly important focus of public debate in an age of digitally accessible pornography. As the question of pornography's relationship to knowledge about sex remains of key interest in public and academic debate – given the recognition that, for many young people, pornography is a key part of their sex education (Litsou et al., 2021) – we also included the domain 'Education about sexual practice'. 'An understanding of consent' was also ranked as being highly important by Delphi panel members – and consent has likewise become an increasingly important part of public debate not only about pornography but also about healthy sexuality more generally, so we included that domain. 'Awareness and acceptance that sex can be pleasurable' was ranked second by members of the Delphi panel. Based on our knowledge of research about sex education we knew that this is an area where formal sex education often falls down (Allen et al., 2013) and pornography is used by young people to fill the gap, so we also included that domain. We report on our findings about these four domains of healthy sexual development in this book.

Causality and correlation

As touched upon above, we noted in our analysis whether the articles we reviewed claimed that the relationship between the consumption of pornography and domains of healthy sexual development was one of correlation or of causation. Correlation means that two variables are related in some way – that if one increases, so does the other. We do not know which one causes the other, or indeed if there is some other variable related to both of them that drives the change. On the other hand, causality means that one variable has a direct effect on the other. This distinction is vitally important. Correlation does not equal causality. If we show, that people who consume pornography are also more likely to have more gender egalitarian attitudes, for example (Kohut et al., 2016), that doesn't prove that consuming more pornography leads to more gender egalitarian attitudes; it could equally mean that having more gender egalitarian attitudes makes people more likely to consume pornography or that an independent factor explains both. In our systematic review, we counted which articles made explicit claims about causality and also which ones *implied* causality. Implied causality was measured through article references to terms including the 'effect', 'impact' or 'influence' of pornography. To clarify the logic of this analysis: whereas 'the correlation of gender egalitarian attitudes with pornography consumption' means the same as 'the correlation of pornography consumption with gender egalitarian attitudes', it is not true that 'the impact of pornography consumption on gender egalitarian attitudes' means the same thing as 'the impact of gender egalitarian attitudes on pornography consumption'. The language of 'impact' implies a unidirectional causal relationship. Having noted whether the articles claimed causality, we then also checked whether the data presented in the article supported claims of causality. In order to do this we recorded the forms of data-gathering that were used. Qualitative forms of data-gathering, like interviews and focus groups, gather data using words, which are then analysed using methods such as thematic analysis. Quantitative approaches use numbers – surveys are usually quantitative, for example – which can then be analysed using statistical methods. Interviews, focus groups and (to a much greater extent) surveys generally produce evidence of correlation rather than causality. When using an experimental design, by contrast, the research process is conducted in a controlled way so that it can be determined that changes to one variable (dependent) are caused by changes in the other (independent). Mixed-methods approaches use a combination of data-gathering methods. We also noted whether data were a snapshot gathered at a single point in time, or whether data was gathered at several points – called a 'longitudinal' study. Snapshots can only ever offer data about correlations.

A note on terminology

In the first chapter we noted that the research undertaken for the President's Commission – and much subsequent research – used the term 'exposure' to describe the relationship between pornography and its audiences. This term has particularly connotations – as per the Oxford English Dictionary, it describes:

> the action of uncovering or leaving without shelter or defence; unsheltered or undefended condition. Also, the action of subjecting, the state or fact or being subjected to any external influence.
>
> (OED online)

The implications of this language are that pornography is something that people should be defended against and sheltered from. There is no agency in being 'exposed' to something. Similarly, talking about the 'effects' of pornography on audiences suggests that the consumers are passive, and things are being done to them, and minimises differences between consumers (Gauntlett, 1998). By contrast, other words – like 'using' pornography, do allow for agency – they imply an active engagement with the text, that people are choosing to do something with it. Other words have yet other connotations – 'consuming' pornography, for example, has both an etymology of eating that implies taking something into your body, as well as a capitalistic implication of being a 'consumer'.

The authors of this book debated for some time which is the most value-free of these terms; and we finally decided that none of them is neutral in any substantive sense. All of them imply particular ways of thinking about the relationships between pornography and its audiences. For this reason, we decided in this book to use all of the terms at different times, thus allowing the different perspectives on the relationship – user, consumer, exposure, effects – to appear throughout our writing. We should emphasise that, even when the term 'exposure' or 'effects' appears in the book, we are not looking at people 'stumbling across' pornography by accident. We are interested in the intentional use/consumption/viewing/reading and so on of sexually explicit materials.

Notes

1 Some elements of this chapter were originally published in Litsou, K., McKee, A., Byron, P., & Ingham, R. (2020). Productive disagreement during research in interdisciplinary teams: Notes from a case study investigating pornography and healthy sexual development. *Issues in Interdisciplinary Studies, 38*(1–2), 101–125.
2 Advisory Group members were Professors Feona Attwood, Dennis Fortenberry, Cynthia Graham, Clarissa Smith, Rebecca Sullivan and Ine Vanwesenbeeck.
3 Delphi panel members were Peter Alilunas, Brandon Arroyo, Martin Barker, Heather Berg, Amy Bleakley, David Church, Lynn Comella, Ed Donnerstein, William Fisher, Rosalind Gill, Gert Martin Hald, Helen Hester, Katrien Jacobs, Steve Jones, Jane Juffer, Taylor Kohut, Charlotta Löfgren-Mårtenson, Giovanna Maina, Neil Malamuth, Shaka McGlotten, Mark McLelland, Brian McNair, John Mercer, Kimberly Nelson, Lucy Neville, Susanna Paasonen, Constance Penley. Julian Petley, Jim Pfaus, Eric Schaefer, Sarah Schaschek, Lisa Z. Sigel, Aleksandar Štulhofer, Shira Tarrant, Evangelos Tziallas, Thomas Waugh, Ronald Weitzer, Eleanor Wilkinson, Paul Wright and Federico Zecca.
4 See the Introduction chapter for more explanation of each of these domains in relation to healthy sexual development.
5 Intercoder or interrater reliability is the extent to which independent coders evaluate a text or a message and reach the same results.
6 Cohen's kappa coefficient is a statistic used to measure intercoder reliability for qualitative items.

References

Allen, L., Rasmussen, M. L., & Quinlivan, K. (Eds.). (2013). *The politics of pleasure in sex education: Pleasure bound*. Routledge.

Attwood, F., & Smith, C. (2010). Extreme concern: Regulating "dangerous pictures" in the United Kingdom. *Journal of Law and in Society, 37*(1), 171–188.

Braun, V., & Clarke, V. (2006). Using thematic analysis in psychology. *Qualitative Research in Psychology, 3*(2), 77–101. https://doi.org/10.1191/1478088706qp063oa

Gauntlett, D. (1998). Ten things wrong with the media effects model. In R. Dickinson, R. Harindranath, & O. Linné (Eds.), *Approaches to audiences: A reader* (pp. 120–130). Arnold.

Kohut, T., Baer, J. L., & Watts, B. (2016). Is pornography really about "making hate to women"? Pornography users hold more gender egalitarian attitudes than nonusers in a representative American sample. *Journal of Sex Research, 53*(1), 1–11. https://doi.org/10.1080/00224499.2015.1023427

Litsou, K., Byron, P., McKee, A., & Ingham, R. (2021). Learning from pornography: Results of a mixed methods systematic review. *Sex Education, 21*(2), 236–252. https://doi.org/10.1080/14681811.2020.1786362

Litsou, K., McKee, A., Byron, P., & Ingham, R. (2020). Productive disagreement during research in interdisciplinary teams: Notes from a case study investigating pornography and healthy sexual development. *Issues in Interdisciplinary Studies, 38*, 1–2.

McHugh, M. L. (2012). Interrater reliability: The kappa statistic. *Biochemia Medica, 22*(3), 276–282.

McKee, A., & Ingham, R. (2018). Are there disciplinary differences in writing about pornography? A trialogue for two voices. *Porn Studies, 5*(1), 34–43. https://doi .org/10.1080/23268743.2017.1390397

McNeill, D., Garcia-Godos, J., & Gjerdaker, A. (2001). *Interdisciplinary research on development and the environment*. University of Oslo Centre for Development and the Environment.

Nair, K., Dolovich, L., Brazil, K., & Raina, P. (2008). It's all about relationships: A qualitative study of health researchers' perspectives of conducting interdisciplinary health research. *BMC Health Services Research, 8*(1), 110–120. https://doi.org/10.1186/1472-6963-8-110

OED online, definition of exposure. https://www-oed-com.ezproxy.lib.uts.edu.au/ view/Entry/66730?redirectedFrom=exposure#eid (accessed 11 May 2022)

PRISMA. (2015). Preferred reporting items for systematic reviews and meta-analyses. http://prisma-statement.org/

Ressing, M., Blettner, M., & Klug, S. J. (2009). Systematic literature reviews and meta-analyses. *Deutsches Ärzteblatt International, 106*(27), 456–463.

Richters, J. (1997). Doing HIV social research: Travelling in two cultures. *Venereology, 10*(4), 214–261.

3 Defining pornography[1]

Alan McKee, Paul Byron, Katerina Litsou and Roger Ingham

Pornography experts

There already exist some overviews of the existing academic research about pornography and its audiences (see, for example, Wright et al., 2016; Grubbs et al., 2019), but these tend to report on research within one discipline or a group of closely cognate disciplines (for example, social psychology and public health). This project represents the first time that an interdisciplinary group of researchers has reviewed relevant research published across the social sciences and humanities academic disciplines. It is a surprisingly difficult project. Although all academic research is committed to gathering, analysing and reporting on data, the ways in which different disciplines do this can be so fundamentally different that translating results between those disciplines can require learning whole new languages (Klein, 1996, p. 46). Indeed, as mentioned in Chapter 2, the original impetus for this project was a recognition that different academic disciplines were producing quite different findings about the relationships between pornography use and its audiences. We noted that some refereed overviews of research in, say, social psychology could write that '[t]here is ... a strong body of evidence ... establishing a link between exposure to sexually explicit material and engagement in aggressive or violent sexual practices' (Guy et al., 2012, p. 546), and that 'pornography has been linked to unrealistic attitudes about sex, maladaptive attitudes about relationships ... belief that women are sex objects ... and less progressive gender role attitudes' (Horvath et al., 2013, p. 7). By contrast, a researcher in literary studies could write that pornography in the 1980s had an important role in 'teaching women that masturbation was an accepted activity' (Juffer, 1998, p. 73), a vital part of feminist politics; and a media studies professor's analysis noted that pornography can similarly support feminist ideals by offering 'to women the possibility of joining other women in discussing sex and imagining sex' (Smith, 2007). Researchers in different disciplines were coming to conclusions about the

DOI: 10.4324/9781003232032-3

relationship between pornography consumption and healthy sexual development but were producing results that appeared to be very different. This inspired us to put together this project, and to explore the published research about the effects of pornography across all disciplines and explore whether the surface differences were in fact real, and how any actual differences in findings could be explained.

Before we go on to report on our systematic reviews about the relationships between pornography consumptions and various domains of healthy sexual development, it is worth spending some time looking at one of the problematic issues that emerged in trying to talk between disciplines, as a case study for the challenges the project faced: how do you even define pornography?[2]

I know it when I see it

In everyday usage, the term 'pornography' is slippery (Willoughby & Busby, 2016, p. 683). Videos on Pornhub are pornography, obviously. And magazines that show people having sex, are clearly pornography. What about *Playboy* magazine? That's got naked women in it – but they're not actually having sex, and they don't spread their legs to show you their genitals in detail. Still, many people describe *Playboy* as pornography. What about lingerie adverts showing women wearing lacy underwear in sexy poses – could that be pornography (Bailey, 2011)? *National Geographic* magazines with photographs of women from across the world with their breasts exposed (Rose, 2012)? What about a sex education book that includes 'anatomically correct drawings of reproductive organs' (Culp-Ressler, 2014)? In all these cases, at least some people have at some point included them in their definition of pornography.

And that is a problem. In everyday practice we can perhaps get away with the now-infamous approach to defining pornography articulated by Justice Potter Stewart in his opinion in the 1964 case *Jacobellis vs Ohio*:

> I shall not today attempt further to define the kinds of material I understand to be embraced within that shorthand description, and perhaps I could never succeed in intelligibly doing so. But I know it when I see it.
>
> (Stewart, 1964, p. 197)

This approach, commonly shortened to the definition of pornography as 'I know it when I see it', works perfectly well in most everyday contexts. But it does not work for academic research on the relationship between consumers and their pornography – because what different people know as pornography when they see it is not the same (Willoughby & Busby, 2016). And in academic research about the possible effects of pornography, it matters a lot if one academic is talking about Pornhub (and its varied genres) and another is talking about sex education books. Although researchers have sought to understand the relationships between the consumption/use of/exposure to pornography for decades, it is only recently that researchers have sought to operationalise a definition of pornography for use in academic research (p. 678).

Psychologists believe that reaching an agreed definition of a variable is vital for the development of formal theories (Sell, 2018) and psychology researchers have begun to approach a consensus about how to define pornography [sometimes the term Sexually Explicit Material (SEM) is used as a synonym (Downing et al., 2014)], employing definitions that focus on two necessary elements. The first is that pornography is 'explicit' (Wright & Randall, 2012, p. 1410) and includes 'images of exposed genitals and/ or depictions of sexual behaviors' (Morgan, 2011, p. 520) that are 'unconcealed' (Peter & Valkenburg, 2011, p. 751). The second is that pornography is 'intended to increase sexual arousal' (Morgan, 2011, p. 520).

However, even within the discipline of psychology there is little agreement about elements of this definition. Some researchers will include in their definition of pornography texts[3] that show only 'nudity' with no sexual contact (Wright & Randall, 2012, p. 1410). By contrast, other researchers in psychology insist that in order to be explicit, pornographic texts must show sexual acts or '(aroused) genitals' (Peter & Valkenburg, 2011, p. 751) – researchers in the latter group exclude *Playboy* from their definition of pornography, for example (Træen & Daneback, 2013, p. e42). In relation to the second part of the definition, some psychology researchers exclude the intention to arouse and include all sexually explicit materials in their definition of pornography (Wright & Randall, 2012, p. 1410; Træen & Daneback, 2013, p. e42). And it is notable that, even in recent work, many researchers do not provide a definition of pornography at all (Hald et al., 2013; Downing et al., 2014; Doornwaard et al., 2015). Given the lack of consensus within a single discipline, it is not surprising that, when we begin to consider other disciplines that are interested in the consumption of pornography, there are even more pronounced disagreements. Researchers in humanities disciplines insist on the heterogeneity of the category and the variety of texts that can function as pornography, including the complicated relationship the category has with other kinds of culture like art or sex education. They point out that texts that are produced for other purposes are used by consumers for pornographic purposes – such as shoe catalogues used as masturbatory aids by foot fetishists (Rose, 2012, p. 549). Indeed, an influential account of pornography by literary historian Kendrick insists that pornography is 'not a thing but a concept, a thought structure' (Kendrick, 1996, p. xiii)

– different cultures at different times categorise different texts as pornographic as a way to control forms of knowledge and thus power relations between groups. For Kendrick, pornography does not have '*any* common qualities' (Williams, 1989, p. 11, italics in original).

The first survey we sent to our Delphi panelists (see Chapter 2) included a question asking everyone to provide an open-ended definition of pornography. A later question in the survey also asked: 'In your professional opinion, what is the relationship of pornography with its audiences/users/consumers, etc?' – drawing out further complexities to the definitions given, as will be discussed. Panel members were also asked to indicate both the discipline in which they conducted their doctoral research, and their current research discipline. Thirty-six of our panel members, working from a range of disciplines, offered a definition of pornography. No two researchers gave exactly the same definition. Over three-quarters of the 36 respondents who attempted this task included the term 'explicit' within their definition for example:

- sexually explicit media;
- the explicit representation of sexual activity, broadly defined, in images and words;
- sexually explicit materials within different media and art formats.

Just over half included 'intention to arouse' or a similar phrase; examples include:

- material designed to provide arousal and entertainment of a sexual nature;
- material that is designed to provoke urges to masturbate;
- an aesthetic work with the primary artistic intention to encourage sexual arousal or other forms of autoerotica;
- explicit sexual representation for the purpose of arousal.

Over half of the sample mentioned only one term or the other, and less than half included both these terms (or cognates) in their definitions. Some of the participants who offered a definition including both elements (or cognates) also added *caveats* to their definition; these included the use of qualifiers such as 'porn often contains', or the use of 'and/or' to link explicitness and arousal, or providing alternative definitions alongside this one – for example:

pornography can be understood in two ways: 1) ... sexual explicitness and/or a purposive attempt to arouse ... 2) ... a frequently disparaging label applied to media texts possessive of a particular set of character-istics such as affectivity, transgressiveness and prurience.

Researchers disagreed on the place of 'intent' in the definition. Some did state that pornographic material must be 'designed', 'produced', 'for the purpose of' or 'aiming at' or 'intended' to or 'meant' to provide arousal. However, other researchers suggested that material is pornographic if it is 'consumed' for sexual arousal, or 'stimulates' or 'sexually arouses'.

So far in our analysis the answers look quite coherent. There might be slight differences in emphasis or language, but they are gesturing at least in the same basic direction. But of course, things are not that simple.

Another group of respondents did not use the language of explicitness, or intent to arouse, at all. Instead, they presented a completely different kind of definition of pornography. They insisted that pornography is not a 'thing' but an 'argument' or a 'process'. The six respondents in the latter camp comprised five who nominated either their doctoral degree or current area of study as film studies or media studies, and one historian. Two mentioned the genre theories of Altman, whereby the content of a genre is the result of a 'contract' between producers and 'a community of users – audiences, fans, critics, etc'; for example:

> I tend to consider pornography as an audio-visual genre; therefore I'd extend to pornography the semantic-syntactic-pragmatic approach developed by Rick Altman. In this sense, I consider pornography as a complex set of semantic elements (for instance, but not exclusively, explicit sex), syntactic elements (specific plot structures, or visual styles, etc.) and pragmatic elements (in this case, the existence of a community of users – audiences, fans, critics, etc. – that considers a specific object as pornographic).

Two mentioned Kendrick's history of pornography, which argues that pornog-raphy is an 'argument' or a 'process, not a thing' as illustrated in the following

> I would hesitate to define it, suggesting as Walter Kendrick does that 'pornography' names an argument, not a thing.
> I tend to go with (and expand) Walter Kendrick's definition: Pornography is a process, not a thing. That process involves cultural shifts, norms, regulations, social relations, taboos, and sanctioned/unsanctioned pleasures and desires.

As Kendrick points out, for example, it was unproblematic in the 19th cen-tury for educated rich white men to view 'erotica', because they were thought to be able to control their reactions and appreciate this material in appropriate ways; but when it became widely available through cheap printing to the uneducated masses it was renamed as 'pornography' and had to be controlled.

So, we found two distinct approaches to the definitions of pornography from our expert panel; the first is a group of answers in the form of 'Sexually explicit materials intended to arouse', or similar formulations which imply an essence to pornography – all pornographic texts will have similar characteristics under this definition (although even here we note that there will be disagreements – is a topless photo of a woman in *Playboy* 'sexually explicit'? If not, is it not pornography?). The second approach is quite different – it's a culturally mediated one which states that at a given time, in a given culture, there will be rules about what is and what is not pornographic, but that these rules can change. At some points in time the category 'pornography' will include only sexually explicit materials intended to arouse but, at other times, other kinds of texts will be included in the category of pornography and 'sexually explicit texts intended to arouse' may not be captured in the category. Arguments about which texts should be included in the category of pornography become power struggles – as we can see in fights about, for example, whether sex education textbooks (McKee, 2017) or artworks (Simpson, 2011) are pornographic.

On the basis of these responses, we identified two (what we thought would be) incompatible themes in the definitions of pornography offered by researchers; these were:

- Sexually explicit materials intended to arouse;
- Pornography is not a thing but a concept, a category of texts managed by institutions led by powerful groups in society in order to control the circulation of knowledge and culture, changing according to geographical location and period.

We then did a second survey of the panel members, offering these two alternative definitions of pornography and asking them to rate their level of agreement with each of them on a five-point scale from 'Strongly disagree' to 'Strongly agree'. All 44 Delphi panel members who enrolled in the study (including those who did not complete the first survey) were invited to participate. Twenty-seven of our experts completed this second survey. Asking our panel members to rate these definitions on a five-point scale, rather than simply asking if they agree or disagree, allowed them to indicate partial agreement; for example, if they agreed with some aspect(s) of the definition but not all of them.

Of the 27 participants who replied to this survey, 21 agreed or strongly agreed with the first definition – *Sexually explicit materials intended to arouse* – while just two disagreed or strongly disagreed. For the second definition, 15 respondents agreed or strongly agreed, while nine disagreed or strongly disagreed. Using a value of 1 for Strongly Disagree through to 5 being Strongly Agree, the mean scores for the two definitions were 4.19 for definition 1, and 3.50 for definition 2.

This finding surprised us at first. We thought that the definitions – one being a strict definition of media content and its intended use, the other recognising culturally contingent aspects that make a single definition untenable – were mutually exclusive. That is clearly not the case. And as we think about it more we see that it makes perfectly good sense to say that the nature of pornography changes between cultures and times – but, at this point in time in Western cultures, pornography means 'sexually explicit materials intended to arouse'.

We also dug down a bit deeper into the responses to see if there were differences between social scientists and humanities researchers. As we mentioned in the Introduction, one of the reasons we started this project in the first place was our sense that there are different silos of academic knowledge about pornography that are developing quite independently from each other. Researchers in one discipline are asking different questions, relying on different assumptions – and yes, using different definitions – from researchers in other disciplines, and there are few points where these distinct bodies of knowledge regularly meet up. So, we were interested to see whether experts from different disciplines responded in different ways to these two definitions. The mean levels of agreement for definition 1 (material intended to arouse) were 4.30 for social scientists and 2.70 for humanities researchers. Corresponding figures for definition 2 (not a thing but a concept) were 4.13 and 4.00 respectively. In other words, social scientists were more likely to agree with both definitions (4.30 and 4.13 respectively), whereas humanities researchers were more inclined to agree with definition 2 (4.00) than with definition 1 (2.70). Further exploration of the ratings revealed that just over half of the 27 participants were in agreement with both definitions.

The fact that researchers across disciplines did not agree on a single definition of pornography is both unsurprising and surprising. It is unsurprising in that several recent researchers have made the same point (Rose, 2012; Andrews, 2012). But it remains a surprising finding that researchers have been gathering data about the relationships between pornography and its consumers for five decades now, yet they have done so without an agreed definition of the object of study. The results of the first round of the survey show that more than half of surveyed researchers used each of the terms 'explicit' and 'arouse', which might offer some hope that 'Sexually explicit content intended to arouse' could offer a starting point for a definitional consensus. But, as we note, only a minority of panellists used both of these terms without *caveats*. We also note the disagreement among researchers as to whether pornographic material must be created with the intent to arouse or whether it is defined by the fact it is consumed to create arousal. The complexity of the different definitions that can be created through different applications of explicitness and/or arousal (with the latter term having two possible meanings – intent to arouse or use for arousal) leads to a complex matrix of definitions, each of which produces a different object of study. One respondent mentioned both explicitness and intent to arouse – and then noted that under their definition this would exclude *Playboy*, as it is does not contain 'clear and explicit acts'. Another mentioned only that material must be explicit, and not that it be designed for sexual arousal – which could include artworks. Another respondent included material designed for sexual arousal, even if not explicit – which could include romance novels, for example. One excluded both explicitness and intent, defining pornography as 'Any material ... that sexually arouses people' – which, they note, would include some of the pictures in *National Geographic* among other materials that are not produced for masturbatory purposes.

Talking across disciplines

So – where do we go from here? We've included this case study to suggest the kinds of challenges that we face as we try to summarise the research about pornography and its audiences that has been produced across a range of academic research. If we cannot even start by deciding on a single definition of pornography, where do we go?

There exists a significant tradition of academic research exploring the challenges of working across disciplines and the ways in which we might address these. Repko and Szostak (2020) suggest that epistemic disagreements between disciplines can be organised under three headings: concepts, theories and assumptions and that assumptions can include:

> what constitutes truth, what counts as evidence or proof, how problems should be formulated and what the general ideals of the discipline are.
>
> (np)

In addition, researchers from different disciplines can face differences in language, including the way key concepts are understood (Szostak, 2013, p. 50). There also may be differences in beliefs and assumptions, differences in identifying the problem (p. 20), and differing epistemologies – for example, critical/contextual or positivist/general (p. 23). Pohl et al. (2008) propose three modes of collaboration among experts from different disciplines that can lead to integration of knowledge – 'common group learning' where team members learn from each other through the process, 'deliberation among experts', where 'team members with relevant expertise … amalgamate their views … during one or more rounds of exchange', and 'integration by a subgroup or individual' where one team member, or a subgroup, takes responsibility for the integrative aspects of the project (p. 415). Three particular aspects of interdisciplinary work have become important for this project.

The first insight is that we must make peace with the fact that the data from different disciplines cannot simply be synthesised into a single coherent whole because some of it might be inconsistent – because of different definitions, different aims and different methods. This does not mean that we have to give up on the process of drawing research together, but it does mean that the process can involve a degree of messiness as well as creativity (Keestra, 2017, p. 121).

A second important insight is that researchers can address differences in language by 'deliberately using everyday language and avoiding scientific terms' (Pohl et al., 2008, p. 415), or by using 'new and redeployed terminology' as the basis for a 'working interlanguage or metalanguage' as with 'pidgin' or 'creole' (Klein, 2012, np). Related to the first point, in order to bring together the insights of different disciplines, which may have conceptualised their objects of study in quite different ways, it is necessary to accept a level of imprecision that is unusual and perhaps unsettling for some academic researchers. This helps explain the tone of this book: we have deliberately used everyday language wherever possible. This decision has a number of advantages. The topic of pornography's effects on its audiences is of interest to a lot of people who may not have formal research training – politicians, journalists and parents for example – and using everyday language wherever possible allows this book to be accessible to these stakeholders. But research discussions of interdisciplinarity also point to the important theoretical rationale behind this decision, allowing the synthesis of results across disciplines.

The third important insight from interdisciplinary researchers is the 'principle of *iteration*': that is, 'moving back and forth … triangulation … reflective balance and weaving together perspectives' (Klein, 2012, np). This means accepting that our findings are always provisional; that we have reached an uneasy truce about what the data across disciplines show but that as we keep talking to our colleagues in different disciplines, translating across our different languages, our insights will change even if the data remain the same (we go into more detail about this process in Litsou et al., 2021).

In relation to our project, we decided in the end that the complex pattern of responses about defining pornography suggests that rather than a single definition of pornography, if we employ *both* definitions we are more likely to meet the needs of an interdisciplinary cohort of pornography researchers. For researchers in disciplines that typically insist on having a single agreed-upon definition before research projects can start, this might be a challenging idea. But in practice, it works. For researchers who are interested in what gets defined as pornography by different people, in different cultures, at different times, for different reasons, it is enabling to define pornography as:

> Pornography is not a thing but a concept, a category of texts managed by institutions led by powerful groups in society in order to control the circulation of knowledge and culture, changing according to geographical location and period.

Such an approach remains true to lived complexity, but fails to produce final, agreed operational terms that allow for replicable research on the audiences of pornography.

However, if we want to produce replicable data – such as through surveys and content analysis – then we need to agree on a definition of the object being studied, even if that definition is understood to be imperfect or incomplete. Allowing for researchers to choose the definition that suits their project represents a pragmatic – and messy, and creative – approach to the problem of defining pornography. Indeed, we think we can see some evidence in our Delphi panel responses that many researchers are already, in practice, balancing a tension between complexity and operational necessity. Twenty-eight panelists provided a definition of pornography that included the terms 'explicit' and/or 'intended to arouse' (or cognates). In a later question, panelists were asked 'In your professional opinion, what is the relationship of pornography with its audiences/users/consumers etc?'. In response to this question 20 respondents – despite presenting a workable operational definition of pornography – included terms that insisted on complexity and variability, such as 'It's many things', 'That really does depend entirely on the circumstances', or 'Complex, and contingent upon many factors'. One researcher who defined pornography as 'sexually explicit visual or printed material that is consumed for sexual arousal', also stated that the relationship between pornography and its consumers is 'Too diverse to sum up neatly, there are so many different kinds of pornography and so many different consumers!' In each of these cases a researcher is aware of the fact that a simple definition of pornography cannot do justice to the complexity of its reality, but is willing to make a contingent decision to lay out a simple definition in order to allow empirical data-gathering to take place and resultant data to be published and hopefully cited. And, by settling on a definition, researchers also increase the possibility of communication with other researchers who may work within other disciplines; even if that communication takes the form of disagreement, at least there is something to talk about.

Having established our definition(s) of pornography, we then looked at the existing academic knowledge about the relationships between consuming pornography and various aspects of healthy sexual development. The next chapter explains what we found about pornography and one of the most important of these: the understanding and practice of sexual consent.

Notes

1 Some elements of this chapter were originally published in McKee, A., Byron, P., Litsou, K., & Ingham, R. (2020). An interdisciplinary definition of pornography: Results from a global Delphi panel. *Archives of Sexual Behavior*, *49*(3), 1085–1091. https://doi.org/10.1007/s10508-019-01554-4.
2 For the formal refereed version of these data see McKee, A., Byron, P., Litsou, K., & Ingham, R. (2020). An interdisciplinary definition of pornography: Results from a global Delphi panel. *Archives of Sexual Behavior*, *49*(3), 1085–1091. https://doi.org/10.1007/s10508-019-01554-4.
3 In this book we use the word 'texts' in the sense in which it is used by cultural studies researchers – that is, any element of culture that carries meaning for a consumer. This can include books, films and photographs as well as T-shirts, coffee mugs or even hairstyles, to name only a few possibilities: McKee, A. (2003). *Textual analysis: A beginner's guide*. Sage.

References

Andrews, D. (2012). Toward a more valid definition of "pornography". *Journal of Popular Culture 45*(3), 457–477.

Bailey, R. (2011). *Letting children be children: Report of an independent review of the commercialisation and sexualisation of childhood* (Vol. 8078). The Stationery Office, London UK.

Culp-Ressler, T. (2014). California parents complain that sex ed textbook is "equivalent to pornography". *ThinkProgress*. Retrieved December 14, 2021, from https://archive.thinkprogress.org/california-parents-complain-that-sex-ed-textbook-is-equivalent-to-pornography-b4a6421d5b7b/

Doornwaard, S. M., van den Eijnden, R. J. J. M., Ovedrbeek, G., & ter Bogt, T. F. M. (2015). Differential developmental profiles of adolescents using sexually explicit internet material. *Journal of Sex Research*, *52*(3), 269–281. https://doi.org/10.1080/00224499.2013.866195

Downing, M. J., Schrimshaw, E. W., Antebi, N., & Siegel, K. (2014). Sexually explicit material on the internet: A content analysis of sexual behaviors, risk and media characteristics in gay male adult videos. *Archives of Sexual Behavior*, *43*(4), 811–821. https://doi.org/10.1007/s10508-013-0121-1

Grubbs, J. B., Perry, S. L., Wilt, J. A., & Reid, R. C. (2019). Pornography problems due to moral incongruence: An integrative model with a systematic review and meta-analysis. *Archives of Sexual Behavior, 48*(2), 397–415. https://doi.org/10.1007/s10508-018-1248-x

Guy, R. J., Patton, G. C., & Kaldor, J. M. (2012). Internet pornography and adolescent health. *Medical Journal of Australia, 196*(9), 546–547. https://doi.org/10.5694/mja12.10637

Hald, G. M., Kuyper, L., Adam, P. G. C., & de Wit, J. B. F. (2013). Does viewing explain doing? Assessing the association between sexually explicit materials use and sexual behaviors in a large sample of Dutch adolescents and young adults. *Journal of Sexual Medicine.* https://doi.org/10.1111/jsm.12157

Horvath, M. A. H., Alys, L., Massey, K., Pina, A., Scally, M., & Adler, J. R. (2013). *Basically ... porn is everywhere. A rapid evidence assessment on the effect that access and exposure to pornography has on children and young people.* Project Report. Office of the Children's Commissioner for England, London, UK.

Jacobellis v. Ohio 378 US, Justice Stewart concurring, (1964).

Juffer, J. (1998). *At home with pornography: Women, sexuality and everyday life.* NYU Press.

Keestra, M. (2017). Metacognition and reflection by interdisciplinary experts: Insights from cognitive science and philosophy. *Issues in Interdisciplinary Studies, 35*, 121–169.

Kendrick, W. (1996). *The secret museum: Pornography in modern culture.* University of California Press.

Klein, J. T. (1996). *Crossing boundaries: Knowledge, disciplinarities and interdisciplinarities.* University Press of Virginia.

Klein, J. T. (2012). Research integration: A comparative knowledge base. In A. F. Repko, W. H. Newell, & R. Szostak (Eds.), *Case studies in interdisciplinary research* (pp. np). Sage Publications.

Litsou, K., McKee, A., Byron, P., & Ingham, R. (2021). Productive disagreement during research in interdisciplinary teams: Notes from a case study investigating pornography and healthy sexual development. *Issues in Interdisciplinary Studies, 38*(1–2), 101–125.

McKee, A. (2003). *Textual analysis: A beginner's guide.* Sage Publications.

McKee, A. (2017). Introduction to volume IV part 1 pornography and pleasure in the classroom. In P. Aggleton (Ed.), *Education and sexualities* (Vol. IV, pp. 2–8). Routledge.

McKee, A., Byron, P., Litsou, K., & Ingham, R. (2020). An interdisciplinary definition of pornography: Results from a global Delphi panel. *Archives of Sexual Behavior, 49*(3), 1085–1091. https://doi.org/10.1007/s10508-019-01554-4

McNeill, D., Garcia-Godos, J., & Gjerdaker, A. (2001). *Interdisciplinary research on development and the environment.* University of Oslo Centre for Development and the Environment.

Morgan, E. (2011). Associations between young adults' use of sexually explicit materials and their sexual preferences, behaviors and satisfaction. *Journal of Sex Research, 48*(6), 520–530. https://doi.org/10.1080/00224499.2010.543960

Peter, J., & Valkenburg, P. M. (2011). The influence of sexually explicit internet material on sexual risk behavior: A comparison of adolescents and adults. *Journal of Health Communication: International Perspectives, 16*(7), 750–765. https://doi.org/10.1080/10810730.2011.551996

Pohl, C., van Kerkhoff, L., Hadorn, G. H., & Bammer, G. (2008). Integration. In G. H. Hardon, H. Hoffmann-Riem, S. Biber-Klemm, W. Grossenbacher-Mansuy, D. Joye, C. Pohl, U. Wiesmann, & E. Zemp (Eds.), *Handbook of transdisciplinary research* (pp. 411–424). Springer.

Repko, A. F., & Szostak, R. (2020). *Interdisciplinary research: Process and theory.* Sage Publications.

Rose, D. E. (2012). The definition of pornography and avoiding normative silliness: A commentary adjunct to Rea's definition. *Philosophy Study, 2*(8), 547–559.

Sell, J. (2018). Definitions and the development of theory in social psychology. *Social Psychology Quarterly, 81*(1), 8–22.

Simpson, B. (2011). Sexualizing the child: The strange case of Bill Henson, his 'absolutely revolting' images and the law of childhood innocence. *Sexualities, 14*(3), 290–311. https://doi.org/10.1177/1363460711400809

Smith, C. (2007). *One for the girls! The pleasures and practices of reading women's porn.* Intellect Books.

Szostak, R. (2013). The state of the field: Interdisciplinary research. *Issues in Interdisciplinary Studies, 31*, 44–65. https://doi.org/10.7939/R3QB9V49Q

Træen, B., & Daneback, K. (2013). The use of pornography and sexual behaviour among Norwegian men and women of differing sexual orientation. *Sexologies, 22*(2), e41–e48. https://doi.org/10.1016/j.sexol.2012.03.002

Williams, L. (1989). *Hard core: Power, pleasure and the 'frenzy of the visible'.* University of California Press.

Willoughby, B. J., & Busby, D. M. (2016). In the eye of the beholder: Exploring variations in perceptions of pornography. *Journal of Sex Research, 53*(6), 678–688. https://doi.org/10.1080/00224499.2015.1013601

Wright, P. J., & Randall, A. K. (2012). Internet pornography exposure and risky sexual behavior among adult males in the United States. *Computers in Human Behavior, 28*(4), 1410–1416. https://doi.org/10.1016/j.chb.2012.03.003

Wright, P. J., Tokunaga, R. S., & Kraus, A. (2016). A meta-analysis of pornography consumption and actual acts of sexual aggression in general population studies. *Journal of Communication, 66*(1), 183–205. https://doi.org/10.1111/jcom.12201

4 Pornography and consent[1]

Alan McKee, Katerina Litsou,
Paul Byron and Roger Ingham

Pornography and consent

Consent has been increasingly recognised as a central component of healthy
sexual development and sexual practice in public debates (Bashan &
Berkovic, 2021) and in sex education (Whittington, 2021).[2] There is ongoing public concern about pornography's impact on sexual health, respectful
relationships and issues of consent (Waterson, 2019). Consent has become
increasingly integrated in public discussions about healthy sex and relationship practice, particularly in relation to identifying and preventing sexual
harassment and sexual assault (Fischel, 2019). Many commentators are
concerned that the consumption of pornography is related to consumers'
understandings and practices of sexual consent (see, for example, Tankard
Reist, 2021).

So – after 50 years of academic research, do we know whether people
who consume more pornography have better or worse understandings of,
and practices of, sexual consent? Surprisingly, after analysing the academic
research on this topic, we found that the answer is: we don't really know,
because that isn't what the research has focused on. This might relate to the
issue of sexual consent only gaining recent traction in sexualities education,
yet sexual consent has been part of this discussion for more than two decades now (Gilbert, 2018).

We might be surprised by this – we would think that this would be a central topic of interest for researchers, given the vital importance of consent.
But what we found in relation to this domain is that researchers have not
paid as much attention as we should to consent as a key aspect of healthy
sexual development. In our focus on pornography research, discussion of
consent often falls within research about pornography's relationship with
sexual violence. And much of this research does not distinguish between
non-consensual violence, and consensual practices of BDSM, kink, spanking, role playing and rough sex. This complicates things.

DOI: 10.4324/9781003232032-4

In reviewing pornography research about consent, we started off by finding the relevant academic articles, as detailed in the 'Search and Analysis Protocol' and searched all relevant peer-reviewed journal articles. In this, and all subsequent searches, we used search terms suggested by two or more of the panel members:

porn* OR "sexually explicit material" OR "visual sexual stimuli"	AND	consent* OR rape OR coercion OR unwanted OR violen* OR aggress* OR assault OR objectif* OR force* OR submiss*

We used this extensive list of terms so that we would pick up research about non-consensual behaviours like rape, or sexual assault, as well as those that explicitly talked about consent. The initial search, after removing duplicates, returned 678 articles. Of these, 576 were excluded after screening of title and abstract and a further 68 were excluded after full texts were reviewed. In total, 34 articles were identified as providing relevant, original data about the relationship between the consumption of pornography and sexual consent and were thus included for analysis. A table providing details of all included articles is available at http://bit.ly/3l5XCIp. We then analysed the articles, as laid out in the Search and Analysis Protocol. We also reviewed the instruments (e.g. surveys) used in each article. For some of the included papers the authors used validated measurement scales, for other papers the authors produced their own questions and some papers reported on qualitative methods, using either focus groups or interviews. Some of these measures were about intentional violence such as rape while others were about the possibility of committing sexual violence. Our analysis of the instruments used found that authors took no consistent approach towards consent, including whether or not they measured consent at all. Indeed, many articles did not measure aspects of consent, but discussed it or made claims about it anyway. In all of our analyses, given the interdisciplinary nature of this project, we were particularly interested in the ways in which articles from social sciences and humanities disciplines approached the topic differently. In relation to this domain of healthy sexual development, though, all of the articles we found originated from social science disciplines. Nevertheless, it became clear in our thematic analysis that our interdisciplinary approach remained important; humanities researchers have written extensively about normative approaches to sexuality, and this became an important theoretical perspective for making sense of the academic research that has been conducted in this area.

Incorrect claims of causality

The journals in which most of the articles were published are *Violence Against Women* (four articles) and *Violence and Victims* (three articles). Following these, two articles were included from each of the following journals: *Aggressive Behavior*; *Archives of Sexual Behavior*; *Psychology of Men and Masculinity*; *Sex Roles*; and *Sexual Addiction and Compulsivity*. This gives some insight into the types of research discussions offered in relation to pornography and matters of consent. Initial coding revealed that, of the 34 articles, 29 report on data collected from a single point in time. Three articles use data collected at more than one time point, and one was based on an experimental design. Data were mostly collected through surveys only (25 articles) with five articles using interviews and/or focus groups. Three articles used mixed methods. Twenty-six of the articles report correlations (as explained in Chapter 2).

However, despite the fact that the data reported actually showed correlations, we found that 19 of the articles *explicitly* claim that pornography causes changes in other variables despite the fact that data were not available to support this claim. Twenty articles *imply* causality – implied causality was measured through article references to terms including the 'effect', 'impact' or 'influence' of pornography (some articles both claimed causality explicitly and also implied it, which is why the numbers add up to more than 34).

Based on our analysis, only 14 of the 34 articles avoid incorrectly claiming or implying causality. This is a breathtaking finding. Despite the fact that academics are trained from the beginning of their careers to avoid incorrect claims about causality, the majority of these research papers about pornography consumption and consent gets it wrong.

We found no agreement in the sample articles about the definition of pornography, what constitutes a suitable taxonomy of kinds of pornography or measures of pornography consumption (see Kohut et al., 2020). The articles refer to at least 13 different kinds of pornography, some overlapping, some referring to medium (e.g. 'internet' pornography), and others to content: 'violent', 'hardcore', 'sadomasochistic', 'rape', 'erotica', 'gonzo', 'violent/degrading', 'softcore', 'mainstream', 'degrading', 'adult-child sex' and 'child'.

We also note that none of the articles attempted to define consent. Despite this being a key aspect of healthy sexual development, we found no work that employed indicators to measure the sophistication of consumers' understanding of how sexual consent should operate.

Themes about pornography consumption and consent

In our qualitative thematic analysis of the articles, our first finding is that

There is no agreement in the literature as to whether consumption of pornography is correlated with better or worse understandings of sexual consent including having attitudes accepting of sexual violence, or likelihood of bystander interventions in cases of sexual violence or coercion.

We made a distinction between people's *understanding* of sexual consent and their *practice* of it. Consent is a complex concept and gaining consent can be a complex process. It is not the case that if someone says 'yes', then all sexual negotiation is completed. Someone can say yes to one particular sexual act – a blow job, perhaps – without agreeing to others – toe-sucking, maybe. Consent can be withdrawn or negotiated at any time during a sexual act. Consent need not be verbal – but consent via body-language can be ambivalent or uncertain. Consent should be free from coercion – so if someone says yes to sex because they are frightened their partner will hit them, that clearly isn't consent. What if they say yes because they're afraid their partner will leave them, even if the partner hasn't said that? What if they say yes because they think it will put their partner in a good mood, and thus more likely to load (or unload) the dishwasher – is that consent?

So, we were interested to find out what we know about whether people who consume pornography have more or less sophisticated understandings of, and attitudes towards, sexual consent. However, we struggled to identify a consistent set of findings in this group of articles. Some articles found correlations between pornography use and attitudes towards sexual consent. One found a correlation between women viewing pornography and being less likely to intervene as a bystander during a sexual assault, and more likely to believe rape myths (Brosi et al., 2011); another found that men who viewed pornography – when compared with those men who did not watch pornography – were less likely to say they would intervene as a bystander, more likely to rape a woman if they were assured they would not get caught or punished and more likely to believe rape myths (Foubert et al., 2011). Another article found a correlation between pornography use and attitudes supporting violence against women, but only for men who are at high risk for sexual aggression and are self-reported frequent consumers of pornography (Malamuth et al., 2012).

However, other articles found that exposure to non-violent pornography had no effect on bystander willingness to intervene, nor to bystander efficacy; while exposure to violent pornography for men but not for women was correlated with bystander willingness to intervene but not to 'bystander efficacy' (Foubert & Bridges, 2017) – that is, the perceived ability to intervene as a bystander. Others found no effect on rape myth acceptance or attraction to sexual aggression after exposure to violent and degrading pornography

(Isaacs & Fisher, 2008), no link between pornography use and attitudes towards sexual coercion (Tomaszewska & Krahé, 2016) and no relationship amongst men (not women) between reading pornographic magazines and aggressive sexual attitudes (Taylor, 2006).

Our second finding from the thematic analysis was:

There is no agreement in the literature as to whether consumption of pornography is correlated with better or worse practices of sexual consent including practising sexual violence or taking bystander actions in cases of sexual violence.

Similar to our findings in relation to the consumption of pornography and sexual consent *attitudes*, there were no consistent findings in relation to pornography use and sexual consent *practices*. Some articles suggest that there is an association between men being sexually aggressive (this did not always specify non-consensual practices, so may involve consensual kink practices) and using pornography (pornography generally, not just violent pornography) (Gwee et al., 2002; Bonino et al., 2006; Vega & Malamuth, 2007; Simons et al., 2012; D'Abreu & Krahé, 2014; Mikoriski & Szymanski, 2017). For example:

> adolescents who use pornography seem more likely to establish relationships with their peers characterized by greater tolerance towards unwanted sexual behaviour.
>
> (Bonino et al., 2006, p. 281)

> frequent corporal punishment in the family of origin combined with consumption of pornographic materials increased the probability that males reported engaging in coercive sexual practice.
>
> (Simons et al., 2012, p. 381)

> Our finding supports assertions about links between rape and pornography.
>
> (Gwee et al., 2002, p. 54)

Another article found a correlation between women's pornography use and all forms of sexual aggression except physical violence and intimidation, though the authors do admit that not enough information was collected about the types of pornography used and the context of its use (e.g. alone or with a partner) (Kernsmith & Kernsmith, 2009). Other articles found a relationship between the use of violent pornography and sexual aggression, but not between the use of non-violent pornography and sexual aggression (Baer et al., 2015). These distinctions between types of pornography are useful context; however, it is not always clear what 'violent pornography' refers to, and there is ongoing disagreement about this among researchers, as discussed below. Furthermore, other articles found no relationship between viewing 'violent and degrading' pornography and self-reporting of sexual coercion or aggression (Gonsalves et al., 2015), or between pornography exposure and sexually aggressive behaviours (Burton et al., 2010).

Why is the data so confusing?

The research on this topic is confused by the fact that, although the everyday use of terms like 'sexual violence' assumes that this means non-consensual behaviour, this isn't always true in the academic research. Some academic research counts consensual practices as being violent; some doesn't. Baron and Richardson, for example, define violence as: 'Any form of behaviour directed toward the goal of harming or injuring another living being who is motivated to avoid such treatment' (1994, p. 37) – emphasising that, in order to be violent, an act must not be consensual. But other definitions exclude consent from consideration, counting any acts that might cause harm as violence, regardless of consent. For example, Stanko's (2001) 'often-cited definition of violence' (Ray, 2011, p. 7) describes it as:

> any form of behaviour by an individual that intentionally threatens to or does cause physical, sexual or psychological harm to others or themselves.
>
> (Stanko, 2001, p. 316)

In this definition, consent is not relevant – 'violence' can be consensual but is still called 'violence' if it can cause physical harm. Under this definition, consensual BDSM could count as violence. Therefore, the history of academic research on pornography and violence/aggression does not map neatly onto research on pornography and sexual consent. It is no wonder, in this context, that the research on pornography consumption and consent is confusing. Indeed, we even found evidence of academic research where consent was framed as negative; for example, Walker et al. write that pornography shows 'violence' where 'female actors displayed eagerness or willingness to comply' (Walker et al., 2015, p. 201) which is framed as a negative behaviour. This seems worrying to us. Consent is at the heart of healthy sexual practice: to exclude it from research is problematic. Take, for example, the work of Bridges et al. analysing 'aggression' in pornography videos (Bridges et al., 2010). They quite explicitly ignore consent from their definition of aggression because paying attention to consent 'results in the rendering of aggressive acts as invisible' when they are consensual (p. 1067). Instead, they take an approach where some sexual acts are always counted as negative 'aggression' whether they are consensual or not – for example spanking. And, conversely, some sexual acts, like kissing, are always counted as 'positive' – again, whether they are consensual or not (p. 1077). From their perspective, then, it can be said that a forced kiss is more 'positive' and less 'aggressive' than a consensual spanking. We do not agree with such a perspective.

Consent is a vital part of sexual health. Our review shows that it has not traditionally been a major focus of pornography research, often being replaced by a focus on 'violence' that does not pay attention to consent. An alternative tradition of research looks at coercion rather than violence (Gonsalves et al., 2015; Tomaszewska & Krahé, 2016). Coercion may not involve physical aggression, but could involve actions such as:

> 'telling them what they want to hear'; saying nice things about the victim or saying that s/he is special; telling them 'it will be good'; proposing marriage; and promising that it will not be 'just one time' … saying mean things; criticizing the victims or calling them 'mean'; questioning their heterosexuality; comparing them to past partners; accusing them of cheating; crying or pouting; making them feel guilty; threatening to stop loving the victim; saying that the victim has stopped loving them.
>
> (Kernsmith & Kernsmith, 2009, p. 596)

This latter approach is directly related to consent, whereas work on aggression or violence sometimes includes consent and sometimes excludes it. This makes coercion a better focus for research into the relationship between the consumption of pornography and sexual health, as opposed to research focusing on violence, which we found to give inconsistent attention to sexual consent.

Normative pornography research

Why does some previous pornography research assume that consensual kinky sex is negative? We suggest that this is part of a larger trend that we noticed in our studies: over the past 50 years, research into the relationships between pornography and its audiences has been profoundly normative. Rather than focusing on healthy sexual development, it has focused on conservative definitions of how people *should* live their sex lives.

In the 1990s, anthropologist Rubin (1992) wrote about the 'charmed circle' (p. 281) of sexual practices that Western cultures approve of:

Sexuality that is 'good', 'normal' and 'natural' should ideally be heterosexual, marital, monogamous, reproductive and non-commercial. It should be coupled, relational, within the same generation, and occur at home. It should not involve pornography, fetish objects, sex toys of any sort.

(pp. 280–281)

A lot of pornography research has been anti-kink; it has called consensual BDSM 'aggression' and argued that it should be stamped out, and that pornography is bad for showing consensual kink. This approach to pornography devalues sex that is unmarried, casual, non-procreative, commercial, in groups, cross-generational, in public, uses pornography, involves manufactured objects or is sadomasochistic, for example.[3] Rubin argues strongly that favouring dominant forms of sexuality over their marginalised counterparts is not scientific or natural, but rather that these 'hierarchies of sexual value':

function in much the same ways as do ideological systems of racism, ethnocentrism and religious chauvinism. They rationalize the well-being of the sexually privileged and the adversity of the sexual rabble.

(p. 280)

Rubin also draws attention to the fact that the production of such hierarchies is imbricated in 'sex negativity' – the tendency to treat sex with suspicion and regard it as requiring excuses such as love or marriage. We argue that the articles in this sample – which privilege 'vanilla' sex over kink – are taking a 'charmed circle' approach. They are not interested in whether the consumption of pornography leads to consensual, happy sex that happens to be kinky; they seem more concerned about whether pornography is correlated with the 'charmed circle' of married, vanilla, monogamous sex. By doing so, these researchers (whether or not they realise it) exclude consent from discussions of healthy sex. Conversely, we believe that consent is central to healthy sexual development, and that attention to consent warrants further discussion within pornography research.

Another issue that has been the focus of much public debate is the fact that young people are using pornography as a form of sex education. What are they learning about sex? And how does it compare with what they are taught in traditional sex education by schools and parents? This is the focus of our next review, reported on in the next chapter.

Notes

1 Some elements of this chapter were originally published in McKee, A., Litsou, K., Byron, P., & Ingham, R. (2021).

2 For the formally refereed version of this data see McKee, A., Litsou, K., Byron, P., & Ingham, R. (2021). The relationship between consumption of pornography and consensual sexual practice: Results of a mixed method systematic review. *Canadian Journal of Human Sexuality*, *30*(3), 387–396. https://doi.org/https:// doi.org/10.3138/cjhs.2021-0010.

3 This is also indicative of heteronormativity – a concept devised by Warner (1991) that builds on the work of Rubin and other queer theorists. A key feature of heteronormativity is the way it erases or devalues sexual cultures and representations that do not fit into expected norms, as per the norms identified in Rubin's charmed circle (perhaps confusingly, heteronormativity has nothing to do with heterosexuality per se – gay sex can be heteronormative; and sex between a man and woman can challenge heterosexual ideals). Pornography research that excludes a discussion of consent while classing consensual acts/ representations of BDSM as violent is heteronormative. As many queer theorists have argued, the social penalties ensured by heteronormativity, and the systems that uphold and enshrine sexual norms (for example, legal, medical and educational systems), are themselves enacting violence.

References

Baer, J. L., Kohut, T., & Fisher, W. A. (2015). Is pornography use associated with anti-woman sexual aggression? Re-examining the confluence model with third variable considerations. *Canadian Journal of Human Sexuality*, *24*(2), 160–173. https://doi.org/10.3138/cjhs.242-A6

Baron, R. A., & Richardson, D. R. (1994). *Human aggression* (2nd ed.). Plenum Press.

Bashan, Y., & Berkovic, N. (2021, May 26). 'Grey area' of sex consent laws clarified. *Australian*, 3.

Bonino, S., Ciairano, S., Rabaglietti, E., & Cattelino, E. (2006). Use of pornography and self-reported engagement in sexual violence. *European Journal of Developmental Psychology*, *3*(3), 265–288. https://doi.org/10.1080 /17405620600562359

Bridges, A. J., Wosnitzer, R., Scharrer, E., Sun, C., & Liberman, R. (2010). Aggression and sexual behavior in best-selling pornography videos: A content analysis update. *Violence Against Women*, *16*(10), 1065–1085. https://doi.org/10 .1177/1077801210382866

Brosi, M. W., Foubert, J. D., Bannon, R. S., & Yandell, G. (2011). Effects of sorority members' pornography use on bystander intervention in a sexual assault situation and rape myth acceptance. *Oracle: The Research Journal of the Association of Fraternity/Sorority Advisors*, *6*(2), 26–35.

Burton, D. L., Leibowitz, G. S., & Howard, A. (2010). Comparison by crime type of juvenile delinquents on pornography exposure: The absence of relationships between exposure to pornography and sexual offense characteristics. *Journal of Forensic Nursing*, *6*(3), 121. https://doi.org/10.1111/j.1939-3938.20010.01077.x

D'Abreu, L. C. F., & Krahé, B. (2014). Predicting sexual aggression in male college students in Brazil. *Psychology of Men and Masculinity*, *15*(2), 152–162. https:// doi.org/10.1037/a0032789

Fischel, J. J. (2019). *Screw consent: A better politics of sexual justice*. University of California Press.

Foubert, J. D., & Bridges, A. J. (2017). Predicting bystander efficacy and willingness to intervene in college men and women: The role of exposure to varying levels of violence in pornography. *Violence Against Women, 23*(6), 692–706. https://doi .org/10.1177/1077801216648793

Foubert, J. D., Brosi, M. W., & Bannon, R. S. (2011). Pornography viewing among fraternity men: Effects on bystander intervention, rape myth acceptance and behavioral intent to commit sexual assault. *Sexual Addiction and Compulsivity, 18*(4), 212–231. https://doi.org/10.1080/10720162.2011.625552

Gilbert, J. (2018). Contesting consent in sex education. *Sex Education, 18*(3), 268–279. https://doi.org/10.1080/14681811.2017.1393407

Gonsalves, V. M., Hodges, H., & Scalora, M. J. (2015). Exploring the use of online sexually explicit material: What is the relationship to sexual coercion? *Sexual Addiction and Compulsivity, 22*(3), 207–221. https://doi.org/10.1080/10720162 .2015.1039150

Gwee, K. P., Lim, L. E. C., & Woo, M. (2002). The sexual profile of rapists in Singapore. *Medicine, Science and the Law, 42*(1), 51–57.

Isaacs, C. R., & Fisher, W. A. (2008). A computer-based educational intervention to address potential negative effects of internet pornography. *Communication Studies, 59*(1), 1–18. https://doi.org/10.1080/10510970701849354

Kernsmith, P. D., & Kernsmith, R. M. (2009). Female pornography use and sexual coercion perpetration. *Deviant Behavior, 30*(7), 589–610. https://doi.org/10 .1080/01639620802589798

Kohut, T., Balzarini, R. N., Fisher, W. A., Grubbs, J. B., Campbell, L., & Prause, N. (2020). Surveying pornography use: A shaky science resting on poor measurement foundations. *Journal of Sex Research, 57*(6), 722–742. https://doi .org/10.1080/00224499.2019.1695244

Malamuth, N. M., Hald, G. M., & Koss, M. (2012). Pornography, individual differences in risk and men's acceptance of violence against women in a representative sample. *Sex Roles, 66*(7–8), 427. https://doi.org/10.1007/s11199 -011-0082-6

McKee, A., Litsou, K., Byron, P., & Ingham, R. (2021). The relationship between consumption of pornography and consensual sexual practice: Results of a mixed method systematic review. *Canadian Journal of Human Sexuality, 30*(3), 387–396. https://doi.org/10.3138/cjhs.2021-0010

Mikoriski, R., & Szymanski, D. M. (2017). Masculine norms, peer group, pornography, Facebook and men's sexual objectification of women. *Psychology of Men and Masculinity, 18*(4), 257–267. https://doi.org/10.1037/men0000058

Ray, L. (2011). *Violence and society*. Sage Publications.

Rubin, G. (1992). Thinking sex: Notes for a radical theory of the politics of sexuality. In C. S. Vance (Ed.), *Pleasure and danger: Exploring female sexuality* (pp. 267–319). Pandora/Harper Collins.

Simons, L. G., Simons, R. L., Lei, M.-K., & Sutton, T. E. (2012). Exposure to harsh parenting and pornography as explanations for males' sexual coercion and

females' sexual victimization. *Violence and Victims*, *27*(3), 378–395. https://doi
.org/10.1891/0886-6708.27.3.378

Stanko, E. (2001). Violence. In E. McLaughlin & J. Muncie (Eds.), *The sage dictionary of criminology* (pp. 315–318). Sage Publications.

Tankard Reist, M. (2021). Why 'consent' doesn't stand a chance against porn culture. *ABC religion and ethics*. Retrieved April 16, 2021, from https://www.abc.net .au/religion/consent-education-does-not-stand-a-chance-against-pornography /13231364

Taylor, L. D. (2006). College men, their magazines, and sex. *Sex Roles*, *55*(9–10), 693–702. https://doi.org/10.1007/s11199-006-9124-x

Tomaszewska, P., & Krahé, B. (2016). Attitudes towards sexual coercion by polish high school students: Links with risky sexual scripts, pornography use and religiosity. *Journal of Sexual Aggression*, *22*(3), 291–307. https://doi.org/10 .1080/13552600.2016.1195892

Vega, V., & Malamuth, N. M. (2007). Predicting sexual aggression: The role of pornography in the context of general and specific risk factors. *Aggressive Behavior*, *33*(2), 104–117.

Walker, S., Temple-Smith, M., Higgs, P., & Sanci, L. (2015). 'It's always just there in your face': Young people's views on porn. *Sexual Health*, *12*(3), 200–206. https://doi.org/10.1071/SH14225

Warner, M. (1991). Introduction: Fear of a queer planet. *Social Text*, *29*, 3–17.

Waterson, J. (2019, October 17). UK drops plan for online pornography age verification system. *The Guardian*. https://www.theguardian.com/culture/2019/ oct/16/uk-drops-plans-for-online-pornography-age-verification-system

Whittington, E. (2021). Rethinking consent with continuums: Sex, ethics and young people. *Sex Education: Sexuality, Society and Learning*, *21*(4), 480–496. https:// doi.org/10.1080/14681811.2020.1840343

5 Learning from pornography[1]

Katerina Litsou, Paul Byron,
Alan McKee and Roger Ingham

Pornographic sex education

Despite improvements in recent years, many young people still find that the formal sex education offered by schools doesn't give them what they want, including information about how to 'form and maintain healthy relationships; the right to decide whether, when, and with whom to engage in sexual behavior; and the fact that sex should be pleasurable, to name just a few' (Kantor & Lindberg, 2020, p. 145). School-based sex and relationships education is often criticised for being overly biological, often too late and concerned with risk-avoidance rather than admitting that sex is potentially pleasurable (Ingham, 2005; Philpott et al., 2006; Allen, 2012). As one young woman put it in a recent survey, school-based sex education 'doesn't tell us the real stuff about sex' (quoted in Fisher et al., 2019, p. 81).

Where else might young people get information about sex? Ideally parents should be a major part of learning about sex. But young people commonly report that their parents' attempts at sex education are limited, uncomfortable and/or consisted of 'warnings or threats about consequences' (Holman & Koenig Kellas, 2018, p. 365).

But, on the other hand, access to pornography through digital media, along with the ability to use anonymous search and browse, makes it easy for people to regularly engage with sexual media (Paasonen, 2011; Attwood et al., 2015; Spišák, 2016). In such a context it is not surprising that many young people use pornography as a significant source of sex education (Albury, 2014). This has fuelled public concern: just what are young people learning from pornography (Dawson et al., 2019)?

In this chapter we report on our review of the academic literature relating to the third healthy sexual development domain: *Education about sexual*

DOI: 10.4324/9781003232032-5

practice (McKee et al., 2010). In doing so, we focus on the question: do people who consume more pornography know more about how to have sex? As with the previous chapter, we found that despite this being a topic of profound public concern – and despite the plethora of academic research on the relationships between pornography and its audiences – there isn't actually much research on this important topic. Once again, academics have tended to focus on other topics that are not necessarily related to healthy sexual development.

For this domain of healthy sexual development, we followed our Search and Analysis Protocol, using the search terms provided by our Delphi panel for this domain:

porn* OR "sexually explicit material" OR "visual sexual stimuli"	AND	education OR information OR learn* OR knowledge OR "sexual health"

After duplicates were removed we had a list of 692 articles; we screened using the same eligibility criteria that we used for all domains. This process left us with ten articles that gave us original data about what consumers of pornography learn about how to have sex (the full list of articles can be found at http://bit.ly/3DUrm2w).

Learning about how to have sex

In reviewing these articles we identified five main themes about how pornography functions as a source of *education about sexual practice* – or what we'll refer to as 'sex education' from now on.

The first, and most common theme, is that young people are using pornography as a source of information to learn 'how to have sex'. This is perhaps not surprising: sex education in schools often focuses on STIs and pregnancy, or even abstinence-only education. It is rare that formal sex education – or information from parents – focuses on how to actually have sex, or, how to have *better sex* (given that many young people are already sexually active when accessing either pornography or sex education). In formal sex education, young people are more likely to learn about the protein coating of the HIV virus than how to give good cunnilingus, for example (McKee et al., 2014). In this context, it is not surprising that research on pornography's role as sex education frequently mentions that inadequate sexual education, and lack of sexual information about the mechanics of sex, means that pornography is an educator of many young people.

Across the ten articles, pornography was mentioned by participants of the studies as being used for learning about sexual performance, positions and roles; for example, Arrington-Sanders et al. (2015) mentioned that:

> Sexual performance was a key theme that emerged among participants as a reason why they watched [sexually explicit media]. Sexual performance included learning about position and sexual roles in certain positions; how adolescents should act during sexual activity with sexual partners; and how sex should feel.
>
> (p. 602)

Pornography told young people 'what goes where' (Arrington-Sanders et al., 2015, p. 602), 'what to do' (Rosengard, Tannis, Dove, Den Berg, et al., 2012, p. 90) and 'how it works' (Kubicek et al., 2010, p. 251). This includes information about the function of sexual organs, 'how to masturbate and ejaculate' (Arrington-Sanders et al., 2015, p. 601), and sexual roles. In their study of US teenagers from alternative high schools and correctional facilities, Rosengard et al. (2012) cite a 17-year-old woman:

> [Before watching porn] I didn't know that sex was like a penis going into a vagina. I thought it was just like when you hump somebody. Like I used to sit on people's laps and think that I was havin' sex.
>
> (p. 88)

And a 17-year-old man:

> At first I was just humpin' and stuff but and then seein' that you stick it in the hole so it went on from that. I don't know, I thought I was good at it ... I just copied what I seen and since ... like ... like at that time, I thought like anybody who was on TV or tape must be great so I thought I was great and good at it.
>
> (p. 90)

In another of the articles, participants who realised that their knowledge was lacking from personal experiences chose to privately address their 'ignorance' by consulting pornography:

> Participants described risking considerable social embarrassment if they were to ask others about sexual behaviours because their peer group stigmatised anyone who seemed to be ignorant about sex. Thus, online SEM offered participants the opportunity to learn more about these topics without risking embarrassment or loss of status.
>
> (Smith, 2013, p. 69)

Pornography was part of an ongoing process of learning about sex:

> youth described sexual development as a process that occurs over time and not all at once where participants described learning about sexual performance through a series of experiences and experiments to determine what felt enjoyable.
>
> (Arrington-Sanders et al., 2015, p. 603).

Rothman et al. (2015) studied pornography use among 16 to 18-year-olds in the USA and reported that pornography was used to learn sex techniques, including how to perform oral, anal and vaginal sex. A 17-year-old woman explained:

> I never knew how to like, suck dick, basically, and I went on there to see how to do it. And that's how I learned.
>
> (quoted in Rothman et al., 2015, p. 740)

Young people commonly noted the lack of practical sex education at school, particularly in studies of men who have sex with men. In Kubicek et al.'s (2010) study, for example, one participant stated:

> Because there's really no information on [anal sex] ... there's really no strong definition nor strong advice about anal sex. It's usually just through word of mouth or from porn.
>
> (p. 251)

Finally, some respondents talked about using pornography to work out if they were ready to start having sex, as well as pornography's value in helping to relax and feel prepared. For example, Arrington-Sanders et al. reported:

> Youth described watching SEM to determine their readiness to have sex. Participants described if they felt aroused by the sex and that [if] they understood how to perform the sex, they were more likely to be ready to engage in sexual activity. SEM served as a bridge to begin sexual activity by calming nerves about sex and helping them to mentally prepare for initiation of sexual activity.
>
> (p. 602)

Learning about sexual identities and sexualities

As well as learning about the mechanics of sex, research has shown that young people learn about sexual identities and sexualities from watching pornography – the second theme we identified. This includes their own and other people's sexualities, and what they find to be sexually arousing. Studies of same-sex-attracted young men reported that pornography use helped them to realise their sexual orientation. For example, an 18-year-old gay man says:

> I started [sic] straight porn but I noticed that I didn't like it because it had a female in it for real and I didn't like it. It was just something that I would just look at the guy. I watch it but I just look at the guy do the stuff.
>
> (quoted in Arrington-Sanders et al., 2015, p. 602)

In the same study, a 19-year-old gay man says:

> Porn taught me a lot. I first started out with straight porn. Porn actually helped me realize that I was gay. When I was watching porn, it started from just boys and girls but I started looking at the guy more. So then I got interested in two guys and a girl and then it just went to two guys and then to more guys and that's when I noticed, 'Wow, I don't like girls anymore'.
>
> (p. 602)

Some young people's first exposure to gay culture was through watching pornography:

> I started going to gay porn sites and I was like 'That's hot'. So then that's kind of how I got exposure to, I guess, gayness.
>
> (quoted in Kubicek et al., 2010, p. 252)

When schools and parents offer little information about sexual identities, it is unsurprising that young people may learn a lot about this from pornography (as well as using pornography for other reasons, such as pleasure).

Inadequate information through pornography

The third theme we found in the research was that young people stated that pornography did not provide them with adequate sexual health information. Many of the articles reported that participants did not see pornography as useful for learning about sexual health. Indeed, some of the participants took a normative approach (see Chapter 3) when they talked about what they wanted to learn about sex – for example, saying that pornography focussed too much on 'fetish' and 'kinky' behaviours (such as fisting, water sports and bestiality) (Kubicek et al., 2010). One participant said that they:

> only learned dirty stuff because they really do dirty things, not healthy. And I'm like … I would learn nothing positive from those movies.
>
> (quoted in Kubicek et al., 2010, p. 252)

Some respondents mentioned that many porn videos do not use condoms, or more generally provide medical information – about, for example, how to protect from Sexually Transmissible Infections (STIs) and unwanted pregnancies. Castro-Vazquez and Kishi (2002) cite a 16-year-old heterosexual man saying:

> If you ask if I learnt about contraception, I would say, no … but anyway, I would say that all those videos show us about sex, but not about 'etiquette', reproduction, contraception and stuff like that. We see videos to satisfy our sexual desires.
>
> (p. 475)

In this area, formal sex education often does a better job – teaching about using condoms is one aspect that is common to much school-based sex education.

Third person concerns about the 'wrong' lessons from porn

The fourth theme we identified was a concern, both amongst researchers and young people, that consumers might get the 'wrong' lessons from porn. Pornography was described in general as providing unrealistic expectations about sexual encounters. Young people who used pornography were concerned that other consumers (but not themselves) might get the wrong lessons from pornography via a 'third person' effect such as by encountering 'unrealistic' messages about sex, bodies, pleasure and 'risky' sex acts. The third person effect describes a common way of thinking whereby people know or believe that they are too intelligent or well-informed to be influenced by media – but assume that other people (often people who are younger than them) will be influenced (Hald & Malamuth, 2008). Participants in research worried that pornography sent lessons about having sex that was too kinky or rough. Doornwaard et al. (2017) report a 17-year-old man participant as saying:

> Porn is often loveless, women are frequently treated disrespectfully, and the actors do things that aren't comfortable or arousing in real-life.
>
> (p. 1043)

While some participants regard this kind of pornography as being arousing, they question the 'unrealistic' aspects of what they have watched, exemplified by this 16-year-old male participant:

> When I am aroused, pornography is fun to watch. But afterwards I regularly ask myself what I just looked at. Not that I view very absurd stuff, but it often is very unrealistic.

> (p. 1044)

Young women, in particular, reported concerns relating to their self-image, the unlikely scenarios and the unrealistic expectations placed on them through watching pornography (Smith, 2013). Young women who did not watch pornography also stated that they felt insecure about their appearance and their sexual performance (Doornwaard et al., 2017). For example, a 20-year-old said:

> So I'd almost be like pissed if that is how it turned out just because the woman is doing everything that the guy wants to do, and I'm definitely not like that at all.

> (quoted in Smith, 2013, pp. 71-72)

These comments overlap with concerns about 'porn literacy': in the next chapter, we return to the issue of 'unrealistic' representations of sex in pornography and explore what kinds of sex are counted as being 'realistic' in these debates.

A need for more relevant sex education

The final theme we identified in the research about pornography and education is a repeated call by researchers for improved sex education in schools that better addresses the needs of young people. Researchers consistently judged that young people were getting the wrong kinds of lesson about sex from pornography; and wanted to balance that out with better messages provided by schools and parents. Some researchers are keen for schools to focus on traditional 'sexual health' information but to do it better:

> schools need to develop strategies on how to teach students basic and effective search methods on obtaining information pertaining to sexual health on the Internet. This would ensure that students receive comprehensive sexual health information from credible websites.

> (Mattebo et al., 2014, p. 197)

By contrast, other researchers call for a broadening of the scope of sexual education: 'to lean away from only teaching about pregnancy prevention and male erections' (Hesse & Pedersen, 2017, p. 768). They insist on 'the need to improve knowledge about different aspects of sex' (Aggarwal et al., 2000, p. 226). In addition, researchers suggest that specific education for same-sex-attracted young people is required, along with a need for teachers to be well-trained and comfortable in discussing sexual diversity (Kubicek et al., 2010); for example

> More policy level strategies are needed that insure federal funding is allocated to comprehensive sexual health education programs that provide [same-sex-attracted] young men with the skills and information needed to make an informed, responsible, and healthy decisions prior to first same-sex.
>
> (Arrington-Sanders et al., 2015, p. 606)

What we don't know

After reviewing existing pornography research that engages with porn users about issues of sexual education and learning, it seems clear that we still do not have an answer to the question: do people who consume more pornography know more about how to have sex? Or, to focus on a subset of that question – do people who consume pornography know more about how to have *good* sex? Two of our themes – inadequate information through pornography and wrong lessons from pornography – point to concerns among young people that pornography is providing limited or inaccurate information about sex and sexual health. Young people and researchers note that much pornography does not deliver sexual health information. This would seem to be uncontroversial. Most pornography is not designed to deliver sexual health information – it is designed to deliver sexual pleasure. It is designed to be entertainment, not education (McKee, 2012) – even if it does end up serving as *de facto* education for young people because their formal schooling and parents are not going to tell them about how to give a good blow job. We don't find complaints in the literature that pornography is doing a bad job of teaching a variety of different sexual positions, for example. At the moment, at least, it seems that formal sex education and pornography are teaching very different aspects of sex – schools can teach about condom use, while pornography can teach about the infinite varieties of ways to gain sexual pleasure. Perhaps it is for this reason that there is no clear evidence that more formal school-based sex education leads to less reliance on pornography for education. There is only limited cross-national research on this topic. We found one article that reported on work with an Irish university student sample, aged 18–24 years, which showed that satisfaction with school-based sex education was not associated with pornography use as a source of sexual information and that individuals may use pornography for information regardless of their sex education in school (Dawson et al., 2019) – because, no matter how much sex education they're getting in school, it is unlikely to include tips on, for example, how to give a good erotic massage. This does raise the question of whether we think people should learn how to develop skills to enhance sexual pleasure: can we imagine this as part of a formal curriculum? Should parents be giving this advice? Or, if not, do we come back to pornography as the only reasonable place in which such learning can be promoted, or at least accessed?

One article in our sample claimed that pornography was the only available source for men who have sex with men to learn about anal sex, since information about this was not provided through school-based sex education (Kubicek et al., 2010). However, this paper does not provide evidence of specific ways of using pornography, nor whether pornography users gain better sexual knowledge, sexual skills and attitudes in comparison to non-users.

We also note that much of the concern that pornography is giving the 'wrong' lessons about sex is expressed in normative terms (as discussed in the previous chapter) – that pornography teaches people about the existence of 'dirty' sex practices like fisting or watersports, or sex that is for fun – 'loveless' rather than within a loving committed couple. Such an approach reinforces conservative norms about acceptable sexual practice – those sitting within Rubin's 'charmed circle' (Rubin, 1992).

One final note – although we were looking for any articles that addressed learning about sex from pornography, most of the research is focused on young people. We would propose that this is one of the problems with the way in which we conceive 'sex education' in our cultures – as something that is only necessary for young people, as though as soon as you turn 21 there is nothing left to learn about sex. One of the 15 domains of healthy sexual development is 'lifelong learning':

> learning about sexuality does not stop at the point where sexual intercourse begins. Adults continue to learn about their sexuality throughout their lives, improving their knowledge of and attitudes toward their sex lives.
>
> (McKee et al., 2010, p. 17)

Are people who consume pornography later in life more likely to continue their sexual education, exploration and development than people who don't? Unfortunately, we did not find any data on this point. We did search, but only located three articles that vaguely addressed this domain of healthy sexual development.

Having established that there is, as yet, no data about the relationship between pornography consumption and knowing more about sex, we move on to our next, related, domain of healthy sexual development – pornography literacy.

Note

1 Some elements of this chapter were originally published in Litsou, K., Byron, P., McKee, A., & Ingham, R. (2021). Learning from pornography: Results of a mixed methods systematic review. *Sex Education*, *21*(2), 236–252. https://doi .org/10.1080/14681811.2020.1786362.

References

Aggarwal, O., Sharma, A. K., & Chhabra, P. (2000). Study in sexuality of medical college students in India. *Journal of Adolescent Health*, *26*(3), 226–229.

Albury, K. (2014). Porn and sex education, porn as sex education. *Porn Studies*, *1*(1–2), 172–181. https://doi.org/10.1080/23268743.2013.863654

Allen, L., & Carmody, M. (2012). 'Pleasure has no passport': Re-visiting the potential of pleasure in sexuality education. *Sex Education*, *12*(4), 455–468. https://doi.org/10.1080/14681811.2012.677208

Arrington-Sanders, R., Harper, G. W., Morgan, A., Ogunbajo, A., Trent, M., & Fortenberry, J. D. (2015). The role of sexually explicit material in the sexual development of same-sex-attracted Black adolescent males. *Archives of Sexual Behavior*, *44*(3), 597–608. https://doi.org/10.1007/s10508-014-0416-x

Attwood, F., Barker, M. J., Boynton, P., & Hancock, J. (2015). Sense about sex: Media, sex advice, education and learning. *Sex Education*, *15*(5), 528–538. https://doi.org/10.1080/14681811.2015.1057635

Castro-Vazquez, G., & Kishi, I. (2002). 'Nemureru Ko Wo Okosu Mono Dearu': Learning about sex at a top ranking Japanese senior high school. *Sexualities*, *5*(4), 465–486.

Dawson, K., Nic Gabhainn, S., & MacNeela, P. (2019). Toward a model of porn literacy: Core concepts, rationales and approaches. *Journal of Sex Research*, *57*(1), 1–15. https://doi.org/10.1080/00224499.2018.1556238

Doornwaard, S. M., den Boer, F., Vanwesenbeeck, I., van Nijnatten, C. H. C. J., ter Bogt, T. F. M., & van den Eijnden, R. J. J. M. (2017). Dutch adolescents' motives, perceptions, and reflections toward sex-related internet use: Results of a web-based focus-group study. *Journal of Sex Research*, *54*(8), 1038–1050. https://doi.org/10.1080/00224499.2016.1255873

Fisher, C. M., Waling, A., Kerr, L., Bellamy, R., Ezer, P., Mikolajczak, G., Brown, G., Carman, M., & Lucke, J. (2019). *6th national survey of secondary students and sexual health 2018*. La Trobe University. https://doi.org/10.26181 /5c80777f6c35e

Hald, G. M., & Malamuth, N. M. (2008). Self-perceived effects of pornography consumption. *Archives of Sexual Behavior, 37*(4), 614–625. https://doi.org/10.1007/s10508-007-9212-1

Hesse, C., & Pedersen, C. L. (2017). Porn sex vs real sex: How sexually explicit material shapes our understanding of sexual anatomy, physiology and behavior. *Sexuality and Culture, 21*(3), 754–775. https://doi.org/10.1007/s/12119-017-9413-2

Holman, A., & Koenig Kellas, J. (2018). "Say something instead of nothing": Adolescents' perceptions of memorable conversations about sex-related topics with their parents. *Communication Monographs, 85*(3), 357–379. https://doi.org/10.1080/03637751.2018.1426870

Ingham, R. (2005). 'We didn't cover that at school': Education against pleasure or education for pleasure? *Sex Education, 5*(4), 375–388. https://doi.org/10.1080/14681810500278451

Kantor, L. M., & Lindberg, L. D. (2020). Pleasure and sex education: The need for broadening both content and measurement. *American Journal of Public Health, 110*(2), 145–148. https://doi.org/10.2105/AJPH.2019.305320

Kubicek, K., Beyer, W. J., Weiss, G., Iverson, E., & Kipke, M. D. (2010). In the dark: Young men's stories of sexual initiation in the absence of relevant sexual health information. *Health Education and Behavior, 37*(2), 243–263. https://doi.org/10.1177/1090198109339993

Mattebo, M., Larsson, M., Tydén, T., & Häggström-Nordin, E. (2014). Professionals' perceptions of the effect of pornography on Swedish adolescents. *Public Health Nursing, 31*(3), 196–205. https://doi.org/10.1111/phn.12058

McKee, A. (2012). Pornography as entertainment. *Continuum: Journal of Media and Cultural Studies, 26*(4), 541–552. https://doi.org/10.1080/10304312.2012.698034

McKee, A., Albury, K., Dunne, M., Grieshaber, S., Hartley, J., Lumby, C., & Mathews, B. (2010). Healthy sexual development: A multidisciplinary framework for research. *International Journal of Sexual Health, 22*(1), 14–19. https://doi.org/10.1080/19317610903393043

McKee, A., Watson, A.-F., & Dore, J. (2014). 'It's all scientific to me': Focus groups insights into why young people don't apply safe sex knowledge. *Sex Education, 14*(6), 652–665. https://doi.org/10.1080/14681811.2014.917622

Paasonen, S. (2011). *Carnal resonance: Affect and online pornography*. MIT Press.

Philpott, A., Knerr, W., & Boydell, V. (2006). Pleasure and prevention: When good sex is safer sex. *Reproductive Health Matters, 14*(28), 23–31. https://doi.org/10.1016/S0968-8080(06)28254-5

Rosengard, C., Tannis, C., Dove, D. C., van den Berg, J. J., Lopez, R., Stein, L. A. R., & Morrow, K. M. (2012). Family sources of sexual health information, primary messages and sexual behavior of at-risk urban adolescents. *American Journal of Health Education, 43*(2), 83–92.

Rothman, E. F., Kaczmarsky, C., Burke, N., Jansen, E., & Baughman, A. (2015). 'Without porn … I wouldn't know half the things I know now': A qualitative study of pornography use among a sample of urban, low-income, Black and hispanic youth. *Journal of Sex Research, 52*(7), 736–746. https://doi.org/10.1080/00224499.2014.960908

Rubin, G. (1992). Thinking sex: Notes for a radical theory of the politics of sexuality. In C. S. Vance (Ed.), *Pleasure and danger: Exploring female sexuality* (pp. 267–319). Pandora/Harper Collins.

Smith, M. (2013). Youth viewing sexually explicit material online: Addressing the elephant on the screen. *Sexuality Research and Social Policy, 10*(1), 62–75.

Spišák, S. (2016). 'Everywhere they say that it's harmful but they don't say how, so I'm asking here': Young people, pornography and negotiations with the notions of risk and harm. *Sex Education, 16*(2), 130–142. https://doi.org/10.1080/14681811.2015.1080158

6 Pornography and porn literacy[1]

Paul Byron, Alan McKee, Ash Watson,
Katerina Litsou and Roger Ingham

Pornography, literacy, expertise

Do people who consume more pornography have a better understanding of how pornography works as a genre? Do they have a more detailed understanding of the languages of pornography, how it is shot and edited, the meanings that consumers make of it? Are they more familiar with subgenres of pornography, and the similarities or differences between them?[2]

Healthy sexual development requires that we develop *competence in mediated sexuality* – that is, 'skills in accessing, understanding, critiquing and creating mediated representations of sexuality in verbal, visual and performance media' (McKee et al., 2010, p. 8). This ability is more commonly named in academic research as 'media literacy' or 'porn literacy' (Dawson et al., 2020). Our Delphi panel had nominated this as the most important aspect of healthy sexual development in regard to pornography, and so we were particularly interested to find out what the academic research in this area had discovered. It would seem to be common sense that the more pornography people consume, the more literate they will become – after all, when we think about literacy in terms of reading and writing, the more books that are read, and the more writing is practiced, the more literate people become. However, our review of the academic literature showed that this is not how 'porn literacy' is usually defined by researchers; and that we don't have much data about whether consuming more pornography leads to better porn literacy.

For this domain we used the search terms:

porn* OR "sexually explicit material" OR "visual sexual stimuli"	AND	fantasy OR genre OR representation* OR literacy OR play OR convention* OR visual* OR real* OR education

DOI: 10.4324/9781003232032-6

As in our other reviews, our date range was 2000–2017. Because smart-phones arrived in the 2000s, these dates encompass over a decade in which mobile digital media has played a significant role in how pornography is accessed, used, produced and shared. We therefore anticipated discussion of digital media literacies in relation to pornography use, as per a rich schol-arship of 'digital literacies' (Pangrazio, 2018). However, while our initial search yielded 1,127 articles, after reviewing every one of these for rel-evance to the domain of *competence in mediated sexuality*, we found that only seven articles provided original data about the relationships between pornography and its audience in relation to porn literacy (a full list of the articles can be found at http://bit.ly/3xjBPBZ).

The lack of literature in this area might seem surprising, given current public attention to porn literacy. We found articles calling for more porn literacy education for young people, and details of proposed curricula in the area. But we found little data that attempted to measure, record or under-stand young people's porn literacies. Beyond this we note that none of the articles we found provided data that directly addressed our key concern – whether people who consume more pornography have better or worse understandings of how sex in the media, including pornography, works as forms of representation, and as genres with particular rules. This, then, is our important finding: that, despite thousands of pieces of academic research there exists little that addresses the relationships between porn consumption and this aspect of healthy sexual development. Unfortunately – as we'll explain below – this may not be surprising as, for some researchers, 'porn literacy' means teaching young people to avoid pornography – the opposite of what the term 'literacy' means in other contexts.

We note that not all of the articles we reviewed explicitly used the word 'literacy', but they all engage with the question of how well consumers under-stand the rules of this genre. Of the seven articles, five relate to young people (Mattebo et al., 2012; Hald et al., 2013; Smith, 2013; Antevska & Gavey, 2015; Baker, 2016) and two relate to gay men (Mowlabocus et al., 2013; Goh, 2017). None addresses the porn literacy of mature heterosexual people. The articles report on empirical research from the UK, the US, Malaysia, New Zealand, Sweden and Denmark. We found four key themes in the data[3].

The first theme is education – which overlaps with our previous chapter. Researchers found that some people used pornography for education and thus called for more training in porn literacy in order to ensure that consum-ers were not learning the wrong things from pornography. This begins to point to the way in which the term 'porn literacy' is used – not as an exper-tise in the genre, but as a corrective against it.

The second theme is a common reference to 'perceived realism' in this literature. Particularly in the social science literature there is a concern that the more realistic consumers think pornography is, the more likely they are to treat it as a model of sexuality and its expression. Underlying this strand of research is a concern that pornography is not 'realistic', and worries that consumers – and particularly younger consumers – won't be able to tell the difference between pornography sex and sex in reality.

The third theme we named 'fiction/fantasy', and this relates to research showing that consumers think of pornography as fantasy or fiction, rather than an instruction manual, and take pleasure from it both in spite of, and because of, this. This theme demonstrates that engagement with pornography (including among young people) is not done naïvely.

The fourth theme was a focus explicitly on media literacy. A number of articles explored what purposes media/porn literacy education should serve, how it should be developed and how it should be delivered to young people.

Because these four themes overlap and inform each other, we have decided to explore what we found in this domain under a single heading that pulls much of the research together – the belief that pornography is 'unrealistic'. What does that mean? What do consumers say about how 'realistic' pornography is? And what does it have to do with healthy sexual development?

Literacy, media literacy, porn literacy

Literacy is 'the ability to read and write', according to the Oxford English Dictionary. Before 'porn literacy' there was 'media literacy': 'the ability of a citizen to access, analyse, and produce information for specific outcomes' (Aufderheide, 1993, p. 6). Although the term encompasses a range of approaches, media literacy fundamentally means understanding that 'media are constructed, and construct reality' (Aufderheide, 1993, p. 2). Media literacy education emerged in Britain, Canada and Australia in the 1970s (Davis, 1993, p. 20) and, from its earliest days, was understood and taught quite differently from 'print literacy' – as found in the study of English literature, for example. Whereas young people were to be taught to become more literate by appreciating books, they were to be taught to become more media literate in exactly the opposite way – by learning to 'reject' media texts (Albury & McKee, 2013, p. 416). Media literacy training for young people typically took a 'protectionist approach for dealing with the [supposedly] essentially negative impact of popular media' (Davis, 1993, p. 21).

Media literacy programmes evolved and became more sophisticated in their engagement with entertainment media:

> from the 1970s onwards, many researchers in the fields of media and cultural studies have rejected the notion that media texts (and indeed

media genres) have singular meanings. Moreover, these disciplines tend to view media representations of gender, power, race, sexuality, and other aspects of identity as contextual. For example, Stuart Hall … has argued that media representations are not as 'distortions' of an objective reality, but are one aspect of our broader 'meaning making' practice.

(Albury & McKee, 2013, p. 416)

In the 2010s, the concept of 'porn literacy' began to emerge (Albury, 2014). Like 'media literacy' in the 1970s …

These debates on porn education tend to presume that young people aged under 18 should be provided with porn literacy education that promotes critical disengagement from pornographic texts.

(Albury, 2014, p. 173)

For Dawson et al. (2020, p. 10), 'Porn literacy education aims to facilitate youth in thinking critically about the content they see'. For some scholars, this involves thinking beyond the content of pornographic texts, to also think about power, gender, sexuality and a range of other social-cultural aspects at play through (but also beyond) these media texts (Jenkins, 2004). However, much research on young people and pornography tends to isolate pornography from broader media ecologies (Goldstein, 2020). Further to this, a media studies approach to porn literacy can also (but rarely does) address the cinematic, technological and economic aspects of porn and its production and industries (Jenkins, 2004). However, most approaches to porn literacy continue to engage with young people to promote what Albury terms 'critical disengagement', whereby young people are simply taught to list the (perceived) social and personal harms of pornography. This is what Goldstein refers to as 'traditional media literacy interventions' in her argument for a need to move beyond these in relation to porn literacies (2020, p. 59). Our review of the literature suggests that this approach to porn literacy remains dominant: it still aims to train people to reject pornography, not to develop a better understanding of the genre. Also, although media literacy aimed to help students learn to make their own, better media, we found no evidence of this strand of production studies in porn literacy programmes.

Porn literacy and realism

The articles we reviewed were largely congruent with this tradition of work on media literacy and porn literacy. Researchers and interview subjects used this language to express their concerns about pornography:

Perceived realism, that is, the extent to which the consumer perceives the pornographic content as realistic ... has been found to be ... a mediator of the impact of internet pornography consumption on adolescents' instrumental attitudes towards sex [i.e. if they are likely to have casual sex].

(Hald et al., 2013, p. 640)

Pornography is 'very degrading to women and unrealistic' says one female student (quoted in Baker, 2016, p. 220), and Baker's study found that 'about 76.8% of young people reported that they did not think the pornography they had seen offered a realistic representation of typical sexual relationships' (Baker, 2016, p. 223). In another study, a young male participant states: 'pornography on the whole builds on incorrect gender roles. Reality does not exactly look like that' (quoted in Mattebo et al., 2012, p. 42). In summary, Mattebo et al. (2012) note that 'Pornographic messages were described as ... depicting a distorted reality' (p. 40). In a third study, Smith (2013) found that among young porn users interviewed 'negative assessments included ... feeling that SEM portrayed unrealistic sexual behaviors' (p. 70).

This approach to porn literacy – insisting that it is important that consumers be taught that pornography is 'unrealistic' – is common. We do not agree that this is a useful way to think about pornography or porn literacy. In order to explain why this is the case, we need to think about the language of media being 'unrealistic'. When we call a representation 'unrealistic', we automatically imply that there could be a more 'realistic' representation. So – what would a more 'realistic' representation of sex look like?

When we examined what academic research describes as 'unrealistic' sex in pornography we found that researchers commonly described or implied conservative sexual practices as realistic; while progressive sexual attitudes or minority sexual practices were described as unrealistic. For example, Hald and Malamuth (2008) write that 'Pornography, while depicting people actually engaging in sexual acts, often portrays an unrealistic picture of sexuality as it is practiced in real life' (2008, p. 615) referencing as evidence the book *Pornified: How Pornography is Transforming Our Lives, Our Relationships and Our Families* (Paul, 2005). That book argues that 'Unlike women in real life, the girls in pornography seem willing to share themselves with a man' because 'real women aren't nearly as into sex' (p. 43). Pornography is unrealistic, says Paul, because women will, among other acts, 'dominate or act submissive' and they will have 'anal sex, double penetration, or multiple orgasms' (p. 44). Pornography, she argues, 'gives men the false impression that sex and pleasure are entirely divorced from relationships' (p. 80). Hald and Malamuth (2008) also quote Fordham who worries that pornography 'creates unreal (and unrealistic) expectations' about 'frequency of sexual activity [and] the kinds of sex acts performed' (Fordham, 2006, p. 82). We note that neither of these references cited by Hald and Malamuth (2008) is refereed academic research – one is a book by a journalist, the other an unrefereed report prepared for an evangelical Christian organisation. Yet these ideals connect with research approaches to pornography use, particularly when there are concerns about the 'effects' of pornography on young people.

Two other non-peer-reviewed examples that have featured heavily in research discussions of pornography's effect on young people, and therefore influence discussions of young people's porn literacies, are Horvath et al.'s *Basically... porn is everywhere* report (2013), and the *Sexualisation of Young People Review* by Papadopoulos (2010). Horvath et al. write: 'pornography has been linked to unrealistic attitudes about sex; maladaptive attitudes about relationships; more sexually permissive attitudes; greater acceptance of casual sex' and more (p. 7). Papadopoulos writes that pornography 'shapes young people's sexual knowledge but does so by portraying sex in unrealistic ways', and 'online pornography' in particular 'is increasingly dominated by themes of aggression, power and control' (p. 12), citing sadomasochism as an example of 'harmful' or 'extreme' behaviours depicted in online porn (p. 12).

These authors quote these sources in order to suggest that casual sex is unrealistic. Strangely, anal sex, women enjoying sex, and BDSM are somehow rendered fictional too – despite all evidence that these exist in the real world. Minority sexual groups, or non-traditional accounts of sex (for example, sex as healthy and enjoyable for women) seem to be written out of 'reality'. We suggest that this speaks to conservative ideals about gender, sexuality and pleasure that pervade much public concern about pornography (see discussion of Rubin's 'charmed circle' in Chapter 4).

Young people as 'critical' consumers of porn

Reading the data provided in these articles, we got the sense that young people are indeed already 'critical' consumers of pornography – in that, when they are asked by researchers about how porn represents sex, young people routinely criticise it:

> Many participants viewed sexually explicit content with a critical eye in terms of lack of realism, problematic representation of bodies, and other messages conveyed about sexuality.
>
> (Smith, 2013, p. 73)

Mattebo et al.'s (2012) evidence of young people's mediated competencies – framed by them as a 'critical-analytical approach' (p. 46) – includes the following discussion of how participants described pornographic bodies and sex:

> The women were represented as underweight with large breasts. This was viewed as demanding if it became an ideal of how young women should look.
>
> (p. 44)

In these articles, critical engagement is also constituted by questioning the gendered aspects of pornography:

> Messages from society regarding gender equality and public health seem to be in conflict with those from pornography and other media with pornographic messages. Some participants reflected on it and had a critical-analytical approach towards these messages, whereas others did not give it much attention.
>
> (p. 46)

We note here another possible quirk in this data: could we perhaps read this feedback from young people as evidence not of porn literacy, but of cultural literacy – they are aware of dominant discourses about pornography in our cultures and how one is *meant* to talk about it? Or perhaps it could even be interpreted as *academic researcher literacy* – young people know what university researchers *think* they should say, and so they want to perform for researchers that they know the right things to say? This is often referred to as 'social desirability bias' (Grimm, 2010). For example, Mattebo et al. (2012) note that:

> The participants also commented on the lack of contraceptives and expressed opinions of discontent suggesting an ability to critically think in relation to pornographic films and messages.
>
> (p. 46)

How did the young people come to be talking about contraception in relation to pornographic films? What kind of questioning framed those discussions? Did the researchers ask about sexual health knowledge? Did the young people in the research raise this spontaneously? Is that how young people talk about pornography outside of the academic research context? We would argue that a 'critical-analytical approach' is sometimes performed by young research subjects within parameters set by adult concerns about young people's sexual health risks and safeties. Perhaps this is linked to the classist assumptions that permeate many analyses of young people's media literacies, also present in these articles:

> The vast majority of participants in this research were from relatively privileged backgrounds in terms of socioeconomic status and education. This likely influenced their ability to be critical consumers of information generally and SEM specifically.
>
> (Smith, 2013, p. 73)

In claims such as this, competence in mediated sexuality is aligned with 'the educated' young person and so it is presumably the 'less educated' young people that we must focus on – that is, those less likely to demonstrate or recite negative attitudes towards, or perform awareness of the artificiality of, pornography.

Porn literacy as 'reading well'

There are other ways of thinking about porn literacy rather than simply rejecting pornography as unrealistic. Think about other kinds of literacy – for example, literacy about Shakespeare's dramas. Those are clearly not 'realistic'. But if that were the entirety of what a student could tell us about them it would not represent a high level of literacy about Shakespeare. There is more to say about how Shakespeare is put together than simply 'that isn't how people talk in real life'. In his ethnographic article engaging with gay men that appeared as part of our sample, Goh (2017) reflects on how his participants' lived experiences indicated a need for pornography debates 'to adopt a more honest, critical and practical trajectory, rather than a notion of pornography as incontrovertibly exploitative, degrading and destructive' (p. 459). From this perspective, porn literacy would mean a positive engagement with pornography that allows consumers to engage productively with sexually explicit material. We find evidence of this form of porn literacy in each of the two articles that focus on gay men and pornography use. Goh (2017) argues that:

> pornography consumption is understood by gay-identifying men as: a means to perform and make sense of sexuality; a self-validated avenue of pleasure; and a site of interior struggle.
>
> (p. 448)

This suggests an approach to porn literacy that is not simply about rejecting pornography and seeing it as a bad or dangerous object to be avoided or dismissed, but instead (linking back to the previous chapter) proposing that pornography can be – and often is – a source of information about sex. From this perspective, porn literacy includes working out how to learn from pornography in a positive rather than negative way. Under this approach, a porn literacy framework should not simply focus on *what* is read (that is, media content) but *how* it is read (that is, media use), acknowledging that pornography can be *read well* to gain useful information about sex, sexuality and pleasure.

Discussing one of his participants, Goh (2017) argues that porn use helped him 'to increasingly clarify his own sexuality' (p. 454), while another of his participants 'suggests that his own use of pornography can provide crucial points of instruction, reflection and deliberation for himself' (p. 455). Similarly, in the second article engaging with gay men, Mowlabocus et al. (2013) argue that:

> By far the most popular understanding [of porn] was its perceived educational dimension, offering instruction on, and experiences of, gay male sexual practices.
>
> (p. 527)

As one of their participants states:

> when you want to find out about it more, it's kind of like a research tool because you want to find out the right positions to do, the right methods, you know, the right actions, to help … just to help pleasure someone properly, you know. And you kind of … it sounds weird, but you kind of learn that in the back of your head and you keep it there.
>
> (p. 527)

Reflecting on such data, Mowlabocus et al. (2013) argue that 'for many gay men pornography is more than "just" material for masturbation' (p. 530), and also offers the possibility of 'learning new sexual techniques' and assistance toward 'validating a sense of self' (p. 530). Porn literacy here means learning to 'read well', to engage with sexually explicit texts in a productive way.

Digital cultures, 'authenticity' and reading pornography well

We do not think it is a coincidence that we only found evidence of a porn literacy approach as 'reading porn well' in relation to gay men. Many of the debates about pornography's supposed negative effects are based in heterosexual relationships – and even in those rare cases where gay authors argue that pornography damages gay relationships, they often do so by arguing that pornography promotes heterosexual-style gender roles for gay couples (Kendall, 2006). For many reasons (such as a recognition that sex education is not provided for gay men), it is more accepted in these articles that gay men might engage positively with pornography than young straight men, for example. Nevertheless, we would argue that, if we are interested in healthy sexual development, we must take this risk and consider porn literacies and uses more widely.

Such an approach to porn literacy would require researchers, educators, parents and others to take into account young people's engagements with, and understandings of, sexually explicit materials. That would mean paying particular attention to digital cultures of intimacy. It would also mean paying attention to the forms of porn literacy that young people demonstrate beyond simply saying that pornography is negative – including understandings of the various subgenres of pornography and the rules for how they work. Bringing these two ideas together – digital intimacies and an expanded understanding of porn literacies – fundamentally destabilises the discourse that pornography is, in any simple way, 'unrealistic'.

The articles we read are aware that the digital distribution of media is an important part of understanding how pornography works – all citing the internet as providing easy access to pornography. But they don't seem to understand much more about digital media than the fact that it is 'accessible' (Hald et al., 2013, p. 639; Baker, 2016, p. 213). They note 'the availability of sexual content online' (Smith, 2013, p. 62) and the 'presumed universality of pornography consumption' (Antevska & Gavey, 2015, p. 611); or, as a participant from Mattebo et al.'s (2012) study states: 'It is shown everywhere' (p. 43). For most of these articles, claims of prevalence and ease of access are the extent of their reflection on digital cultures of pornography. But there is more to say on this.

One important insight about digital cultures is the increasing importance of 'authenticity' as a virtue in entertainment, in cultural arenas such as social media and amateur pornography (Paasonen, 2011). For Paasonen, these overlapping media genres thrive on depictions of authenticity, even in texts that are obviously constructed and therefore not authentic in the sense of presenting unmediated reality. In other words, 'authenticity' is often an aesthetic strategy. In social media such as Instagram, Snapchat or Tinder, media content is often read as dubious, and sometimes publicly challenged, if it seems too staged, polished, filtered or 'professional' (Duguay, 2017). As such, we can argue (as Paasonen and others do) that amateurism is a logic – one that carries through many sites, including social networking, digital dating, television and pornography – that conveys intimacy. It is also a preference, as well as a genre. Through various digital media practices – informed by digital media literacies and an ongoing development of media themes and genres – 'reading for realness' can filter out risks of inauthenticity in one's everyday media practices (Albury et al., 2019), and this literacy can structure our affective engagement with everyday media as well as our pleasure preferences. Digital media trade in affect – 'intensities of feeling that both precede and give shape to nameable emotions' (Paasonen, 2016, p. 428). Authenticity is a key aspect of DIY/amateur porn being read as intimate and representing ordinary people. On this basis, it can be argued that 'perceived realism' – to re-signify this term – is necessary to incite particular kinds of affect and erotic pleasure for young people. Indeed, many participants in the studies we reviewed did speak to these pleasures, as highlighted below. With this in mind, simply telling young people that (all) porn is 'unrealistic' makes no sense; because many are already involved in a project of looking for sexually explicit material that is more 'authentic'. These discourses of authenticity are important in the ways that young people make sense of the pornography they consume; and this challenges the discourse that pornography is 'unrealistic' in important ways. As Paasonen (2011) observes: 'Amateur porn revolves around notions and promises of real bodies, real pleasures, real people, and real places' (p. 84). Yes, there are rules for representation and how the (sub) genres of pornography work – but just saying it is not 'realistic' barely scratches the surface of those complexities of representation.

When we revisit the data provided in the porn literacy articles with this new perspective, we think we can see evidence that the young respondents show high levels of porn literacy – not in the sense of rejecting all pornography, but in the sense of reading pornography well. They demonstrate a sophisticated and nuanced understanding of how pornography works – perhaps a greater sense of porn literacy than many researchers. For example, several participants in these studies discuss their preference for 'real bodies' and how these are available through DIY and amateur pornography:

> Positive assessments of SEM included that it portrayed a more realistic range of people and bodies than mainstream sexual content and that it provided a safe means of exploring and learning about sexuality.
>
> (Smith, 2013, p. 70)

Participants are aware that what they are seeing is still a representation, but they engage in nuanced discussions about the relationship between performance and authenticity:

> I actually prefer the amateur stuff because I feel like it is more realistic … [people in amateur SEM] are putting on an act, but I think it's also even more of a realistic act than porn from the porn industry. They look more real, they act more real.
>
> (Marion, aged 20, quoted in Smith, 2013, p. 71)

> Amateur porn[ography] does a surprisingly good job of varying everything and so I never felt intimidated or bad about myself while watching it.
>
> (Sophie, age 22, quoted in Smith, 2013, p. 70)

Paasonen argues that pornography's attraction is also about the 'evidence of sexual pleasure captured by the camera' (2011, p. 81). Again, this is linked by young consumers to questions of authenticity, and is evidenced in these articles by the research participants (male and female) who express concerns for the situation of female performers (see, for example, Antevska & Gavey, 2015). For many porn users (including these young people), the pleasure of amateur/DIY porn relies on authenticity, and this is contextualised through critical understandings of pleasure and reality and where these meet. In the context of broader digital media use, a model of porn literacy that simply seeks to label pornography as 'unrealistic' fails to engage with the complexities of understanding realism or authenticity across young people's broader digital media practices. Such an engagement offers a useful elaboration for pornography researchers and sexuality educators who want to better understand, and build upon, young people's porn literacies.

The ability to produce porn well

As we noted above, media literacy historically includes a commitment to 'the ability of a citizen to access, analyze, and *produce* information for specific outcomes' (Aufderheide, 1993, p. 6). We've added emphasis on 'produce' here because it is important to note that in the development of porn literacy out of media literacy the ability to be literate in the 'production' of pornography has fallen by the wayside. We emphasise here that we are not talking about industrial production, training young people to move into careers as professional pornography directors. In a digital context, young people are increasingly producing and circulating their own sexual images, using camera phones, sexting and sharing material with their sexual partners. A focus on how young people engage with digital cultures – and particularly in the importance they place on 'authenticity' – can help us to address that missing element.

Once again, though, our systematic literature review found little existing research on a fundamental question about the effects of pornography: do people who consume porn have a better understanding of the rules of the genre? In the next chapter we explore our final domain of healthy sexual development – awareness and acceptance that sex can be pleasurable – and find yet another surprising gap in the research.

Notes

1 Some elements of this chapter were originally published in Byron, P., McKee, A., Watson, A., Litsou, K., & Ingham, R. (2021).
2 For the formally refereed version of this data see Byron, P., McKee, A., Watson, A., Litsou, K., & Ingham, R. (2021). Reading for realness: Porn literacies, digital media, and young people. *Sexuality & Culture*, *25*(3), 786–805. https://doi.org/10.1007/s12119-020-09794-6.
3 Our profound thanks to our Research Assistant Ash Watson, for her formulation of the key themes for this domain.

References

Albury, K. (2014). Porn and sex education, porn as sex education. *Porn Studies*, *1*(1–2), 172–181. https://doi.org/10.1080/23268743.2013.863654

Albury, K., Byron, P., McCosker, A., Pym, T., Walsh, J., Race, K., Salon, D., Wark, T., Botfield, J., Reeders, D., & Dietzel, C. (2019). *Safety, risk and wellbeing on dating apps: [final report]*. Swinburne University of Technology, Melbourne.

Albury, K., & McKee, A. (2013). Introduction to part III: Sexual cultures, entertainment media and communications technologies. In L. Allen & M. L. Rasmussen (Eds.), *Palgrave handbook of sexuality education* (pp. 415–421). Palgrave Macmillan.

Antevska, A., & Gavey, N. (2015). "Out of sight and out of mind": Detachment and men's consumption of male sexual dominance and female submission in pornography. *Men and Masculinities*, *18*(5), 605–629. https://doi.org/10.1177/1097184X15574339

Aufderheide, P. (1993). *Media literacy. A report of the national leadership conference on media literacy*. The Aspen Insititute, Communication and Society Program, Washington DC 20036. (ISBN-0-89843-137-9) [ERIC Number: ED365294].

Baker, K. E. (2016). Online pornography - should schools be teaching young people about the risks? An exploration of the views of young people and teaching professionals. *Sex Education*, *16*(2), 213–228. https://doi.org/10.1080/14681811.2015.1090968

Byron, P., McKee, A., Watson, A., Litsou, K., & Ingham, R. (2021). Reading for realness: Porn literacies, digital media, and young people. *Sexuality and Culture*, *25*(3), 786–805. https://doi.org/10.1007/s12119-020-09794-6

Davis, J. F. (1993). Media literacy: From activism to exploration. In P. Aufderheide (Ed.), *Media literacy: A report on the national leadership conference on media literacy* (pp. 18–44). The Aspen Insititute, Communication and Society Program, Washington DC 20036. (ISBN-0-89843-137-9) [ERIC Number: ED365294].

Dawson, K., Nic Gabhainn, S., & MacNeela, P. (2020). Toward a model of porn literacy: Core concepts, rationales, and approaches. *Journal of Sex Research*, *57*(1), 1–15. https://doi.org/10.1080/00224499.2018.1556238

Duguay, S. (2017). Dressing up Tinderella: Interrogating authenticity claims on the mobile dating app Tinder. *Information, Communication and Society*, *20*(3), 351–367. https://doi.org/10.1080/1369118X.2016.1168471

Fordham, G. (2006). *"As if they were watching my body": Pornography and the development of attitudes towards sex and sexual behaviour among Cambodian youth, [research report]*. World Vision, Cambodia. https://issuu.com/viva/docs/namecaa5d4

Goh, J. N. (2017). Navigating sexual honesty: A qualitative study of the meaning-making of pornography consumption among gay-identifying Malaysian men. *Porn Studies*, *4*(4), 447–462. https://doi.org/10.1080/23268743.2017.1371066

Goldstein, A. (2020). Beyond porn literacy: Drawing on young people's pornography narratives to expand sex education pedagogies. *Sex Education*, *20*(1), 59–74. https://doi.org/10.1080/14681811.2019.1621826

Grimm, P. (2010). Social desirability bias. In *Wiley international encyclopedia of marketing*. https://doi.org/10.1002/9781444316568.wiem02057

Hald, G. M., & Malamuth, N. M. (2008). Self-perceived effects of pornography consumption. *Archives of Sexual Behavior*, *37*(4), 614–625. https://doi.org/10.1007/s10508-007-9212-1

Hald, G. M., Malamuth, N. N., & Lange, T. (2013). Pornography and sexist attitudes among heterosexuals. *Journal of Communication*, *63*(4), 638–660. https://doi.org/10.1111/jcom.12037

Horvath, M. A. H., Alys, L., Massey, K., Pina, A., Scally, M., & Adler, J. R. (2013). *Basically ... porn is everywhere. A rapid evidence assessment on the effect that access and exposure to pornography has on children and young people*. Office of the Children's Commissioner for England, London, UK. https://eprints.mdx.ac.uk/id/eprint/10692

Jenkins, H. (2004). Foreword: So you want to teach pornography? In P. C. Gibson (Ed.), *More directly looks: Gender, pornography and power* (pp. 1–7). BFI Publishing.

Kendall, C. (2006). Pornography, hypermasculnity and gay male identity: Implications for male rape and gay male domestic violence. In C. Kendall & W. Martino (Eds.), *Gendered outcasts and sexual outlaws: Sexual oppression and gender hierarchies in queer men's lives* (pp. 105–130). Harrington Park Press.

Mattebo, M., Larsson, M., Tydén, T., Olsson, T., & Häggström-Nordin, E. (2012). Hercules and barbie? Reflections on the influence of pornography and its spread in the media and society in groups of adolescents in Sweden. *European Journal of Contraception and Reproductive Health Care*, *17*(1), 40–49. https://doi.org/10.3109/13625187.2011.617853

McKee, A., Albury, K., Dunne, M., Grieshaber, S., Hartley, J., Lumby, C., & Mathews, B. (2010). Healthy sexual development: A multidisciplinary framework for research. *International Journal of Sexual Health*, *22*(1), 14–19. https://doi.org/10.1080/19317610903393043

Mowlabocus, S., Harbottle, J., & Witzel, C. (2013). Porn laid bare: Gay men, pornography and bareback sex. *Sexualities*, *16*(5–6), 523–547. https://doi.org/10 .1177/1363460713487370

Paasonen, S. (2011). *Carnal resonance: Affect and online pornography*. MIT Press.

Paasonen, S. (2016). Visceral pedagogies: Pornography, affect and safety in the university classroom. *Review of Education, Pedagogy and Cultural Studies*, *38*(5), 427–444. https://doi.org/10.1080/10714413.2016.1221711

Pangrazio, L. (2018). *Young people's literacies in the digital age: Continuities, conflicts and contradictions*. Routledge.

Papadopoulos, L. (2010). *Sexualisation of young people*. Crown copyright, ref. 299136. ISBN: 978-1-84987-186-0.

Paul, P. (2005). *Pornified: How pornography is transforming our lives, our relationships and our families*. Times Books.

Smith, M. (2013). Youth viewing sexually explicit material online: Addressing the elephant on the screen. *Sexuality Research and Social Policy*, *10*(1), 62–75.

7   Pornography and pleasure[1]

Alan McKee, Katerina Litsou,
Paul Byron and Roger Ingham

The still, still missing discourse of desire

In 1988, Fine famously wrote about 'the missing discourse of desire' in school sex education, noting that 'The naming of desire, pleasure, or sexual entitlement, particularly for females, barely exists in the formal agenda of public schooling on sexuality' (Fine, 1988, p. 33). In 2006, almost 20 years later, she noted that pleasure in sex education was 'still missing after all these years' (Fine & McClelland, 2006). A 2018 survey of Australian school students suggests that the problem still exists. As one student put it:

> Please teach students that sex is a healthy part of growing up and that they should practice it safely if they want to and they shouldn't feel ashamed of themselves for enjoying it.
>
> (quoted in Fisher et al., 2019, p. 80)

The final domain of healthy sexual development that we report on in this book is pleasure.[2] Our question is simple: do people who consume more pornography have more pleasurable sex lives? The capacity to experience pleasure without shame is a vital part of a healthy sex life, and so understanding the effect of pornography consumption on that is, you would think, vitally important. Surely there has been a lot of academic research conducted on this?

Our search terms for this systematic review were:

porn* OR "sexually explicit material" OR "visual sexual stimuli"	AND	pleasur* OR fun OR satisfaction OR arousal OR orgasm OR recreational OR permissive OR desire OR "role play" OR fantas*

DOI: 10.4324/9781003232032-7

The initial search, after removing duplicates, returned 524 articles. After reviewing these against our criteria 68 articles were identified as providing relevant data about the relationship between the consumption of pornography and sexual pleasure and were thus included for thematic analysis. A table with details of all included articles can be found at http://bit.ly /2JMAhfs.

The journals in which most articles were published were *Archives of Sexual Behavior* (N = 8), *Journal of Sex Research* (N = 3), *Sex Roles* (N = 3) and *Sexologies* (N = 3), each of which publishes articles mainly using methods of data gathering and analysis derived from psychology; and *Porn Studies* (N = 7) and *Sexualities* (N = 3) which are interdisciplinary. Initial coding revealed that, of the 68 papers coded, 58 reported on data collected from a single point in time. Six papers reported data collected at more than one time point, and four were based on experimental designs. Data was mostly collected through surveys only (N = 45) with 11 using interviews and/or focus groups. A minority of articles (N = 7) used mixed methods.

In this review we once again found a lot of mistaken claims for causality (see discussion in Chapter 2). Most of the articles in this sample (42 of 68) reported correlations. In this sample, ten of the articles *explicitly* claimed that pornography *causes* changes in the behaviours of people who use it, despite the fact that the presented data does not support this claim. Another 23 *implied* causality, again without appropriate data. Only 35 of the articles (around half the sample) avoided inappropriately claiming or implying causality. As with our analysis of pornography and consent, the fact that almost half the sample of articles inappropriately claimed or implied that pornography causes changes in behaviours – when in fact the results presented only correlations – is extremely important and represents one of the key findings across this project.

The thematic analysis of these articles identified two key themes: the first relates to pleasure and the second to satisfaction. We report first on the theme of pleasure as that is the focus of this analysis, although the theme of satisfaction was actually more dominant in the sample.

Pleasure

The theme of pornography use and pleasure was organised into two sub-themes. The first subtheme is about masturbatory pleasure resulting from the use of pornography. The second relates to sexual pleasure with partners, and whether pornography use impacts this.

Masturbatory pleasure: We noted at the start of this book that this project was explicitly interdisciplinary. Involving researchers from a variety of humanities and social science backgrounds in this work meant we could include, understand and synthesise the data produced by researchers using quite different methodologies. In some instances, this approach also revealed differences between humanities and social scientific approaches to understanding the relationships between pornography and its consumers – as is the case here. We noticed that research on pornography and pleasure tends to take different forms in the humanities articles reviewed compared with the articles from the social sciences. In humanities research we noticed more engagement with pornography consumers about what pornography they use, why they use it and how that feels. This research presents more context and information from consumers about conflicted feelings in regard to their use of pornography. Such an approach seeks to understand the ways in which consumers make sense of the material they view. The research shows that most consumers take sexual pleasure from their consumption of pornography:

> speaking to the pleasurable aspect of consuming pornography, and in addition to sexual gratification, some participants [young men with non-exclusive sexual orientations] also discussed the importance of 'quality' in their usage. For example, Rory said, 'I will think, "I'm going to find a good video and take a little more time with this and get some release and feel good about that"'.
>
> (McCormack & Wignall, 2017, p. 983)

The research also suggests that sexual pleasure may have some relationship with the development of sexual agency – that is:

> an individual's feelings of empowerment within the sexual domain … sexual agency provides a sense that an individual has the right to create and take action on his or her own behalf, to make sexual choices, and to meet his or her sexual needs.
>
> (Horne & Zimmer-Gembeck, 2005, p. 29)

So, for example, humanities researchers noted of one consumer that:

> Ava also noted how her consumption of online pornography helped her to focus on her own sexual pleasure and to put her own sexual needs first. She explained, consuming SEM [Sexually Explicit Material] online helps her to remember 'my own pleasure is actually of paramount importance'.
>
> (McKeown et al., 2018, p. 347)

This can also be related to the development of sexual identities; in an article that turned up both in our sample for porn literacy, and for our sample of articles on pornography and pleasure, a researcher found that 'gay-identi-fying research participants perceive pornography as a personally validated avenue to pleasure' (Goh, 2017, p. 455).

The articles also reported that, while consumers take pleasure from the consumption of pornography, this can be conflicted because of cultural factors, especially amongst women. Several articles, both from social sciences and humanities, noted a tension between the sexual pleasure that women take from pornography and wider cultural discourses

> Although Julia acknowledges the pleasurable sexual stimulation that pornography offers, she strives to restrict her personal porn use, as it clashes with the accepted cultural script of being 'a good girl'. It seems that awareness of these cultural scripts causes more distress to Julia than the actual pornographic content she consumes.
>
> (Spišák, 2017, p. 365)

> Women's enjoyment of porn, in particular, poses ideological and aesthetic dilemmas ... their pleasures are difficult to reconcile with their reservations.
>
> (Gurevich et al., 2017, p. 577)

Articles in this subtheme tend to focus on women and gay men as consumers of pornography. By contrast, research with heterosexual men overwhelmingly presents their use of pornography – and indeed we might say, heterosexual masculinity itself – as a risk (Szymanski & Stewart-Richardson, 2014). The sample includes no articles that seek to find out whether pornography can serve to increase heterosexual men's experience of sexual pleasure. We noted a similar point in the previous chapter about research on porn literacy, where researchers could imagine gay men 'reading porn well' – but we found no evidence of research taking a similar approach to heterosexual men's engagement with pornography.

When articles from the social sciences do focus on masturbatory pleasure they tend to avoid the term 'pleasure' and instead talk about 'arousal'. These articles generally find that participants are 'aroused' by pornography (Lofgren-Martenson & Mansson, 2010; Reid et al., 2011; Laier et al., 2013), are more 'aroused' by pornography than by neutral films (Glascock, 2005; Staley & Prause, 2013) and that men are more 'aroused' by pornography than women (Glascock, 2005; Lofgren-Martenson & Mansson, 2010). They find pornography is 'used' for purposes including masturbation, mood management, entertainment when bored and as a contributor to sexual practice with a partner (Paul & Shim, 2008; Sun et al., 2016).

Sexual pleasure with partners: A second subtheme – more prevalent in articles from the social sciences – is not about the (masturbatory) pleasure that results from consuming pornography itself, but is rather concerned with how the use of pornography is related to later (non-pornographic) sexual pleasure between people; that is to say, if someone uses pornography for masturbation, does this have an impact on their sexual pleasure with another person? Research falling within this subtheme takes a media effects approach (Bryant & Oliver, 2008) to understand the relationship between pornography and pleasure and tends to position pleasure as a subfactor in relationship/marital satisfaction. As we mentioned in Chapter 2, approaching the relationship between audiences and pornography use as 'effects' tends to minimise or deny the agency of consumers, and differences between them (Gauntlett, 1998). These articles are discussed in more detail under the theme of 'Satisfaction' below.

It is of interest that some of the articles reviewed – primarily from the social sciences – see pleasure itself as risky, or even negative. We can see this, for example, in articles which view masturbation with suspicion:

> Previous research illustrates that some pornography use may be 'auto-erotic sexuality' where one has a sexual experience through masturbation. These autoerotic sexual experiences through pornography use may potentially shape an individual's attitudes that sex is primarily to extend your own pleasure and is strictly physical.
>
> (Brown et al., 2017, p. 468)

As researchers who are committed to sexual health, we note that masturbation often makes an important contribution to healthy sexual development (Coleman, 2002), including – as noted above – in the development of sexual agency. Concerns about the selfishness of masturbation are moral, rather than being about sexual health.

Satisfaction

This brings us to our second theme. Although our primary focus for this domain of healthy sexual development was research on pornography use and pleasure, our systematic review revealed that attention to pleasure was often a secondary theme in the articles we found. Interestingly, and particularly among articles from the social sciences, we found a primary focus on *satisfaction.*

Twenty-one articles in the sample addressed sexual satisfaction, 11 addressed relationship satisfaction and five addressed marital satisfaction.

In total, 37 articles in the sample – more than half – addressed some kind of satisfaction.

Satisfaction is a rough synonym for pleasure; but it is not quite the same thing. Many articles in the sample gathered data about satisfaction using, between them, 13 separate scales to measure 'sexual satisfaction', 'couples satisfaction' and 'marital satisfaction'. By contrast, no scales were used to measure sexual pleasure. Articles in this same category also discuss 'relationship satisfaction' and 'dyadic adjustment' – the latter defined as 'the quality of adjustment in romantic relationships' (Stewart & Szymanski, 2012, p. 262). Other articles are not explicitly about relationship satisfaction, but implicitly link sex with relationships. These articles draw on satisfaction scales which are labelled as measuring 'sexual satisfaction' but which ask questions which firmly position sexual practice within couple-based (and implicitly monogamous) relationships, asking more about relationship quality than sexual pleasure. For example, the Golombok-Rust Inventory of Sexual Satisfaction (Rust & Golombok, 1985) asks 'Are you dissatisfied with the amount of variety in your sex life *with your partner*?' (emphasis added in all quotations); the Global Measure of Sexual Satisfaction (Lawrance & Byers, 1995) is 'used to assess global satisfaction with various aspects of the sexual *relationship*'; the Sexual Satisfaction Questionnaire (Butler et al., 2011) includes statements such as 'I wish that *my partner* would be more experimental/adventurous during sexual activity'; the Multidimensional Sexuality Questionnaire (Snell et al., 1993) includes the item 'My sexual *relationship* is very good compared to most'.

Of the many scales used, only two ask about sexual pleasure independent of emotional intimacy, a dyadic relationship or marriage. The Arizona Sexual Experiences Scale (McGahuey et al., 2000) asks about 'sex drive, arousal, vaginal lubrication/penile erection, ability to reach orgasm, satisfaction from orgasm, and pain during sex' – although it is notable that the authors also feel the need to use 'the Sexual Compulsivity Scale (Kalichman, 2010) and the Sexual Avoidance Subscale of the Sexual Aversion Scale (Katz et al., 1989)', ensuring that the question of sexual pleasure as risk is also present. Snell's Index of Sexual Satisfaction (Snell et al., 1993) measures 'the way in which one's sexual needs are being met, the degree in which one feels sexually fulfilled, and the appraisal of whether something is presently missing in one's sexual life'. Only research from the social sciences wrote about satisfaction; it was not mentioned in humanities research. The relationship between relationship/marital satisfaction and sexual pleasure *per se* is not made explicit in any article in the sample.

One subtheme of writing about satisfaction was that 'Higher frequencies of SEM use were associated with less sexual and relationship satisfaction' (Morgan, 2011, p. 520). Several articles in the sample were interested in this topic and provided similar findings (Stewart & Szymanski, 2012; Poulsen et al., 2013; Perry, 2016). As noted early in this chapter, there is confusion in some articles about the role of causality in the association between pornography use and sexual satisfaction. Even within a single article authors can move between a recognition that causality cannot be assumed and attempts to assume causality. For example, Morgan writes:

> It is important to recognize that SEM viewing frequency either could contribute to lower sexual and relationship satisfaction or a non-satisfying sex-life or relationship might contribute to more frequent SEM viewing.
>
> (Morgan, 2011, p. 528)

But, on the same page, she also writes:

> This difference could reflect a disconnect between their preferences and their actual sexual and relationship experiences, suggesting that SEM viewing may indeed set up young adults to expect unrealistic sexual encounters.
>
> (p. 528)

Many articles in the sample claim or imply causality where they have in fact only demonstrated association:

> It appears that pornography has a negative impact on love and marital satisfaction. The results indicated that love and marital satisfaction had a significant negative relationship with pornography.
>
> (Fadaki & Amani, 2015, p. 245)

> The data was consistent with the notion that more gender role conflict leads to more anxious and avoidant attachment styles which in turn lead to more pornography use which in turn leads to less relationship quality and less sexual satisfaction.
>
> (Szymanski & Stewart-Richardson, 2014, p. 76)

Within this subtheme, researchers also examined the role of a number of intervening variables in the relationship between pornography use and relationship satisfaction, including 'discrepancies' between partners in pornography use rather than simple frequencies of pornography consumption (Willoughby et al., 2016), attachment styles (Gouvernet et al., 2017) and religiosity (Perry, 2016).

The normativity of relationship research

We take a moment here to note that relationship satisfaction is not a necessary part of healthy sexual development. People can have happy healthy sex lives without being in a relationship; and people can be satisfied with their relationships while having no sex. This approach to pornography and sex is, once again, a profoundly normative one. It values stable relationships more than sexual pleasure. It also normalises (monogamous) sex as a necessary part of a dyadic relationship and ignores that many people are asexual (Scherrer, 2008).

All of the articles reviewed addressed, in some form, the question of pornography and pleasure; but the different disciplines involved do so in different ways. As we note above, some of the articles explicitly refer to 'pleasure'; but others used the language of 'arousal'. While these terms may seem to be synonymous, they represent different lenses through which pornography use experiences are viewed. People have and enjoy a range of experiences of pleasure, and this is an important part of healthy sexual development. The pleasure of pornography often involves bodies, such as through masturbation, but it need not. Arousal, however, centres a physiological response to pornography, and this is not necessarily a part of healthy sexual development. It is also interesting to note that in psychology arousal is not a straightforwardly positive term – indeed, in studies of aggression, arousal can be seen as risky and even something to be avoided.

This difference in language points to the different theoretical traditions and research agendas that converge in the field of pornography studies. Once again, different disciplines, our results suggest, are asking different questions about the effects of pornography, or the relationships of audiences with their pornography consumption. For some research traditions, pleasure is something that is seen as worthwhile and important in and of itself, warranting the study of the varied practices and experiences of pleasure, as well as ways in which it can be maximised. For other research traditions, pleasure is side-lined to focus on the satisfaction of marital (or marriage-like) relationships.

A focus on relationships rather than on pleasure in the articles we reviewed is, as we noted above, a normative approach that accepts the 'charmed circle' identified by Rubin (1992), whereby 'Sexuality that is "good", "normal" and "natural" should ideally be ... marital, monogamous, reproductive ... coupled, relational' (pp. 280–281). Relationship-focused research is grounded in the dominant sexual ideology. Rubin also draws attention to the fact that the production of such hierarchies is imbricated in 'sex negativity' – the tendency to treat sex with suspicion and regard it as requiring excuses such as love or marriage. We argue that the articles in this sample which privilege relationship quality over sexual pleasure are taking a 'charmed circle' (and thus, normative) approach. They are not interested in whether the consumption of pornography leads to more masturbatory sexual pleasure; they are interested rather in the association between the consumption of pornography and 'good' stable relationships, measured by way of marital/relationship/couple satisfaction. Conversely, in humanities disciplines such as media and cultural studies pleasure has long been an object of fascination for its potential to disrupt problematic cultural systems such as heterosexual marriage –a patriarchal institution opposed by many feminists (Gotfrit, 1988). These different approaches to pleasure represent more fundamental orientations towards culture – a desire to keep things stable versus a desire for disruptive progressive change.

Another finding from our review of these articles reinforces our suspicion that much pornography research takes a normative approach: because, notably, another theme of these articles is a focus on 'risk' (the next most common theme after pleasure and satisfaction). Mentions of risk appeared in the majority of articles considered (44 out of 68), suggesting that pornography's pleasure is often understood within a risk framework. We coded these mentions of risk into subthemes, and found 'risky sexual behaviours' (or 'sexual risk behaviours') to be the most common. This can refer to particular sexual acts depicted in pornography (for example, unprotected anal intercourse), or sexual behaviours of pornography users, potentially influenced by pornography use (including 'casual sex' and having multiple partners). Other risks commonly discussed include pornography addiction, HIV/STI transmission risks, sexual abuse or aggression and the gendered risks of pornography (specifically the social risks to women who engage with pornography). Some concern was also raised about pornography users 'modelling risk behaviours' or learning about sex through pornography (a concern among researchers that we found in all four of our reviews). Finally, several studies suggested that the internet itself was risky for providing easy access to pornography. We call this approach 'normative' because healthy sexual development does not mean avoiding risk entirely; it means being aware of various risks, and making informed decisions about what ones to take, and how best to mitigate against them. Similarly, there are many risks involved in sex beyond catching STIs – for example, forced abstinence can be 'risky' in that it can lead to mental health difficulties; or being in a heterosexual relationship can be 'risky' for a woman as that greatly increases her chances of being murdered by her intimate partner. None of the articles in our sample that discusses the 'risks' of pornography and pleasure mentioned these kinds of risks. Because abstinence and heterosexual relationships are part of the 'charmed circle', the risks they carry are ignored.

We noted above that articles about pornography and pleasure tend to focus on women and gay men as consumers while research with heterosexual men tends to present their use of pornography as a risk. This reflects the disparate traditions and theoretical paradigms in pornography research, and the fact that different questions tend to be asked concerning different population groups. Traditional 'effects' research focuses on heterosexual men, and is concerned with 'risk', whereas research on women and gay men often enquires into the subjective experience of pornography consumption, and centres on questions of sexual agency and sexual identity development. This is related to the fact that women and men are positioned differently in respect to pornography, and with the differing functions that pornography fulfils in the lives of gay and straight men. We did not encounter any research papers about the use of pornography among lesbian/queer women, which underscores how much of this scholarship is underpinned by (hetero)normative approaches to female sexuality – with researchers often focusing on how this is represented and 'risked' by pornography and its use.

This concludes the substantive chapters of the book. We have presented our analysis of what academic research knows, after 50 years, about the relationships between consuming pornography and four aspects of healthy sexual development – consent, education, literacy and pleasure. To get here we've reviewed thousands of academic journal articles, and engaged in many months of discussion and analysis to find ways to make sense of the data across a variety of disciplinary approaches. It will have been noticed that several recurring themes have emerged in our analysis. In the conclusion we review the four projects, draw attention to the recurring themes – and bring our analysis up to date.

Notes

1 Some elements of this chapter were originally published in McKee, A., Litsou, K., Byron, P., & Ingham, R. (2021).
2 For the formal refereed version of this data see McKee, A., Litsou, K., Byron, P., & Ingham, R. (2021). The relationship between consumption of pornography and sexual pleasure: Results of a mixed-method systematic review. *Porn Studies*, *8*(3), 331–344. https://doi.org/10.1080/23268743.2021.1891564.

References

Brown, C. C., Conner, S., & Vennum, A. (2017). Sexual attitudes of classes of college students who use pornography. *Cyberpsychology, Behavior and Social Networking*, *20*(8), 463–469.

Bryant, J., & Oliver, M. B. (2008). *Media effects: Advances in theory and research.* Routledge.

Butler, M. E., Holm, J. E., & Ferraro, F. R. (2011). Pornography's immediate effect on relationship satisfaction. *Psi Chi Journal of Undergraduate Research, 16*(3), 113–122.

Coleman, E. (2002). Masturbation as a means of achieving sexual health. *Journal of Psychology and Human Sexuality, 14*(2–3), 5–16.

Fadaki, S. M. J., & Amani, P. (2015). Relationship of love and marital satisfaction with pornography among married university students in Birjand, Iran. *Journal of Fundamentals of Mental Health, 17*(5), 240–246.

Fine, M. (1988). Sexuality, schooling, and adolescent females: The missing discourse of desire. *Harvard Educational Review, 58*(1), 29–53. https://doi.org/10.17763/haer.58.1.u0468k1v2n2n8242

Fine, M., & McClelland, S. (2006). Sexuality education and desire: Still missing after all these years. *Harvard Educational Review, 76*(3), 297–338. https://doi.org/10.17763/haer.76.3.w5042g23122n6703

Fisher, C. M., Waling, A., Kerr, L., Bellamy, R., Ezer, P., Mikolajczak, G., Brown, G., Carman, M., & Lucke, J. (2019). *National survey of secondary students and sexual health 2018.* La Trobe University. https://doi.org/10.26181/5c80777f6c35e

Gauntlett, D. (1998). Ten things wrong with the media effects model. In R. Dickinson, R. Harindranath, & O. Linné (Eds.), *Approaches to audiences: A reader* (pp. 120–130). Arnold.

Glascock, J. (2005). Degrading content and character sex: Accounting for men and women's differential reactions to pornography. *Communication Reports, 18*(1), 43–53. https://doi.org/ 10.1080/08934210500084230

Goh, J. N. (2017). Navigating sexual honesty: A qualitative study of the meaning-making of pornography consumption among gay-identifying Malaysian men. *Porn Studies, 4*(4), 447–462. https://doi.org/ 10.1080/23268743.2017.1371066

Gotfrit, L. (1988). Women dancing back: Disruption and the politics of pleasure. *Journal of Education, 170*(3), 122–141. https://doi.org/10.1177/002205748817000308

Gouvernet, B., Rebelo, T., Sebbe, F., Hentati, Y., Yougbaré, S., Combaluzier, A., & Rezrazi, A. (2017). Is pornography pathogen by itself? Study of the role of attachment profiles on the relationship between pornography and sexual satisfaction. *Sexologies, 27*, e27–e33. http://doi.org/10.1016/j.sexol.2016.10.001

Gurevich, M., Brown-Bowers, A., Cosma, S., Vasilovsky, A. T., Leedham, U., & Cormier, N. (2017). Sexually progressive and proficient: Pornographic syntax and postfeminist fantasies. *Sexualities, 20*(5–6), 558–584. https://doi.org/10.1177/1363460716665785

Horne, S., & Zimmer-Gembeck, M. J. (2005). Female sexual subjectivity and well-being: Comparing late adolescents with different sexual experiences. *Sexuality Research and Social Policy, 2*(3), 25–40.

Kalichman, S. C. (2010). Sexual compulsivity scale. In T. D. Fisher, C. M. Davis, W. L. Yarber, & S. L. Davis (Eds.), *Handbook of sexuality-related measures.* Routledge.

Katz, R., Gipson, M., Kearl, A., & Kriskovich, M. (1989). Assessing sexual aversion in college students: The sexual aversion scale. *Journal of Sex and Marital Therapy, 15*(2), 135–140.

Laier, C., Schulte, F. P., & Brand, M. (2013). Pornographic picture processing interferes with working memory performance. *Journal of Sex Research, 50*(7), 642–652. https://doi.org/10.1080/00224499.2012.716873

Lawrance, K.-A., & Byers, E. S. (1995). Sexual satisfaction in long-term heterosexual relationships: The interpersonal exchange model of sexual satisfaction. *Personal Relationships, 2*(4), 267–285.

Lofgren-Martenson, L., & Mansson, S.-A. (2010). Lust, love, and life: A qualitative study of Swedish adolescents' perceptions and experiences with pornography. *Journal of Sex Research, 47*(6), 568–579. https://doi.org/10.1080/00224490903151374

McCormack, M., & Wignall, L. (2017). Enjoyment, exploration and education: Understanding the consumption of pornography among young men with non-exclusive sexual orientations. *Sociology, 51*(5), 975–991. https://doi.org/10.1177/0038038516629909

McGahuey, C., Gelenberg, A. J., Laukes, C. A., Moreno, F. A., Delgado, P. L., McKnight, K. M., & Manber, R. (2000). The Arizona sexual experience scale (ASEX): Reliability and validity. *Journal of Sex and Marital Therapy, 26*(1), 25–40.

McKee, A., Litsou, K., Byron, P., & Ingham, R. (2021). The relationship between consumption of pornography and sexual pleasure: Results of a mixed-method systematic review. *Porn Studies, 8*(3), 331–344. https://doi.org/10.1080/23268743.2021.1891564

McKeown, J. K. L., Parry, D. C., & Light, T. P. (2018). 'My iPhone changed my life': How digital technologies can enable women's consumption of online sexually explicit materials. *Sexuality and Culture, 22*(2), 340–354. https://doi.org/10.1007/s12119-017-9476-0

Morgan, E. (2011). Associations between young adults' use of sexually explicit materials and their sexual preferences, behaviors and satisfaction. *Journal of Sex Research, 48*(6), 520–530. https://doi.org/10.1080/ 00224499.2010.543960

Paul, B., & Shim, J. W. (2008). Gender, sexual affect, and motivations for internet pornography use. *International Journal of Sexual Health, 20*(3), 187–199. https://doi.org/10.1080/19317610802240154

Perry, S. L. (2016). From bad to worse? Pornography consumption, spousal religiosity, gender, and marital quality. *Sociological Forum, 31*(2), 441–464. https://doi.org/10.1111/socf.12252

Poulsen, F. O., Busby, D. M., & Galovan, A. M. (2013). Pornography use: Who uses it and how it is associated with couple outcomes. *Journal of Sex Research, 50*(1), 72–83. https://doi.org/10.1080/ 00224499.2011.648027

Reid, R. C., Li, D. S., Gilliland, R., Stein, J. A., & Fong, T. (2011). Reliability, validity, and psychometric development of the pornography consumption inventory in a sample of hypersexual men. *Journal of Sex and Marital Therapy, 37*(5), 359–385. https://doi.org/10.1080/0092623X.2011.607047

Rubin, G. (1992). Thinking sex: Notes for a radical theory of the politics of sexuality. In C. S. Vance (Ed.), *Pleasure and danger: Exploring female sexuality* (pp. 267–319). Pandora/Harper Collins.

Rust, J., & Golombok, S. (1985). The Golombok-Rust inventory of sexual satisfaction. *British Journal of Clinical Psychology, 24*(1), 63–64.

Scherrer, K. S. (2008). Coming to an asexual identity: Negotiating identity, negotiating desire. *Sexualities, 11*(5), 621–641.

Snell, W. E., Fisher, R. D., & Walters, A. S. (1993). The multidimensional sexuality questionnaire: An objective self-reported measure of psychological tendencies associated with human sexuality. *Annals of Sex Research, 6,* 27–55.

Spišák, S. (2017). Negotiating norms: Girls, pornography and sexual scripts in Finnish question and answer forum. *Young, 25*(4), 359–374. https://doi.org/10.1177/1103308816660482

Staley, C., & Prause, N. (2013). Erotica viewing effects on intimate relationships and self/partner evaluations. *Archives of Sexual Behavior, 42*(4), 615–624. https://doi.org/10.1007/s10508-012-0034-4

Stewart, D. N., & Szymanski, D. M. (2012). Young adult women's reports of their male romantic partner's pornography use as a correlate of their self-esteem, relationship quality and sexual satisfaction. *Sex Roles, 67*(5–6), 257–271. https://doi.org/10.1007/s11199-012-0164-0

Sun, C., Bridges, A., Johnson, J. A., & Ezzell, M. B. (2016). Pornography and the male sexual script: An analysis of consumption and sexual relations. *Archives of Sexual Behavior, 45*(4), 983–994. https://doi.org/10.1007/s10508-014-0391-2

Szymanski, D. M., & Stewart-Richardson, D. N. (2014). Psychological, relational and sexual correlates of pornography use on young adult heterosexual men in romantic relationships. *Journal of Men's Studies, 22*(1), 64–82. https://doi.org/10.3149/jms.2201.64

Willoughby, B. J., Carroll, J. S., Busby, D. M., & Brown, C. C. (2016). Differences in pornography use among couples: Associations with satisfaction, stability, and relationship processes. *Archives of Sexual Behavior, 45*(1), 145–158. https://doi.org/10.1007/s10508-015-0562-9

8 Recent academic research on pornography and healthy sexual development

Alan McKee, Katerina Litsou,
Paul Byron and Roger Ingham

Key findings

We started this book with the moment, around 50 years ago, when the US President's Commission on Obscenity and Pornography provided its *Report* on 'the effect of obscenity and pornography upon the public, and particularly minors, and its relationship to crime and other antisocial behavior' (Commission on Obscenity and Pornography, 1970, p. 1). As we noted in the Introduction, 50 years later academics are still trying to answer many of the same questions, and the issues remain as incendiary as ever. This remains an area where academic knowledge is of fundamental and urgent interest to a range of stakeholders in public debate. Just what do we know about the relationship between the consumption of pornography and healthy sexual development after 50 years of academic research across disciplines? We hope that this book will be a useful resource to anybody who is concerned by, and wants to participate in, these debates.

The book presents the first overview of the literature across academic disciplines: the trends, the contradictions, the findings and the problems in pornography research. Our search process only extends to December 2017, and we are very aware that some important research has emerged since then – some of which we point to below. We also note that, because our research method favoured replicability over exhaustiveness (that is, using a scientific method that can be replicated by others), we may have missed some relevant literature. However, we are confident that our accounts of the broad trends are accurate.

So – after 50 years of academic research, what do we know about the relationship between pornography consumption and healthy sexual development? Our key findings are as follows:

1. Although we can identify thousands of pieces of academic research about pornography's 'effects', surprisingly little of it explores

DOI: 10.4324/9781003232032-8

relationships between various aspects of healthy sexual development and consumption of pornography.

2. A lack of agreement about what is being measured has led to confusion; this includes lack of agreement about the definition of pornography.

3. Much of the relevant research we identified on the relationship between consumption of pornography and aspects of healthy sexual development misinterpreted correlation as causality.

4. There is no agreement in the literature as to whether consumption of pornography is correlated with better or worse understandings or practices of sexual consent, including having attitudes accepting of sexual violence, or the likelihood of bystander interventions in cases of sexual violence or coercion.

5. The literature does not provide data about whether people who use pornography are likely to have more information about how to have (good) sex than people not using pornography. We know that people say they use pornography to learn about sex, but we do not know how formal sex education, parents, friends and sexualised entertainment compare as sources of information about how to have (good) sex.

6. We do not have data about whether people who consume pornography have better levels of porn literacy. We know that some people refer to 'porn literacy' as encouraging young people to reject pornography as 'unrealistic'; we also note an alternative – and we think more useful – approach that takes porn literacy to mean learning how to read porn well.

7. We do not have data about whether people who consume pornography have more or less pleasurable sex lives. We note there is little research on pleasure; there exists more research, particularly from the social sciences, on relationship satisfaction. This seems to show that people who have less satisfying relationships may use more pornography.

8. Much of the research on pornography has been normative; it has assumed that the only healthy form of sexuality is vanilla sex (that is, not kinky) between monogamous couple-based partners for reasons beyond simply pleasure.

Pornography across disciplines

This project draws on published academic research from all social science and humanities disciplines and brings together research that is often quite siloed. This is a unique, and important, approach. The four researchers working on this project have distinct intellectual histories and quite different personalities. Each of us brought different perspectives and skills to the project. We also began to see some trends in the different ways our disciplines have trained us to approach academic research. The researchers trained in the humanities were vigilant for normative discourses, informed by years working with cultural studies approaches and engaging with queer theory. The social science researchers insisted on rigour and set a clear level for the evidence needed to support any claims we made. The humanities researchers argued to expand what we counted as data; the social scientists insisted on what 'traditionally' counts as data. The humanities researchers were obsessive about language choices and written expression; the social science researchers insisted that clarity was more important than beauty or nuance in our writing.

We also noticed, to take a broad-brush approach, that there were some differences between humanities and social scientific research into pornography. It was more common for humanities researchers to study pleasure – with its implications of being disruptive and political – while it was more common for social science researchers to explore relationship satisfaction. Humanities research was more interested in the meanings that consumers made of pornography and more commonly listened to consumers as their own experts about pornography use; social scientific research was broadly less interested in treating pornography consumers as co-creators of knowledge about pornography consumption. We also found that studies more likely to engage with porn consumers and the pleasures and knowledge they gain from pornography were more often reported by qualitative researchers working in humanities disciplines, and that they were more likely to engage with women and gay men about their pornography use, and rarely straight men for whom pornography use was mostly framed as problematic across the broader interdisciplinary literature.

The majority of this book reports on a series of systematic reviews of academic research across disciplines, up to the end of 2017. After designing and implementing the Search and Analysis Protocol in a way that satisfied all the disciplines involved (drawing on consultation with a Delphi panel of experts), we then engaged in repeated iterative discussions about the data that was found, the themes that we identified and how to report on them. It was a lengthy process but guaranteed the robustness of the data that we report on here. In what follows are some examples of more recent research literature (since 2018) that has furthered the conversations offered by this book.

Consent and pornography

The next four sections of this conclusion look at some of the academic research that has been published since the end of our systematic reviews on the relationships between pornography consumption and the domains of healthy sexual development that we studied. These following sections might be called 'unsystematic reviews'; we gathered relevant articles from a range of sources, by searching databases, reviewing our own records of material we have encountered, asking colleagues and snowball sampling – and then identified articles that we thought were interesting or important in relation to pornography consumption and consent, education, literacy and pleasure.

In relation to pornography and sexual consent, recent research addresses a range of variables – such as rape myth acceptance (Maas & Dewey, 2018), coercive behaviours (Stanley et al., 2018) or self-reported inclination towards rape (Palermo et al., 2019). There is no clear pattern in the findings. Some studies find associations between pornography consumption and consent variables (Stanley et al., 2018); some studies find no association (Dawson et al., 2019); others find an association between pornography consumption and one form of non-consensual behaviour but not with others (Maas & Dewey, 2018); and others find no association with non-consensual behaviour measured using one scale, but they do find an association when it is measured using another (de Heer et al., 2020). Some researchers have differentiated between different kinds of pornography, finding an association between only 'violent' pornography (using a definition of violence that excludes consent) and non-consensual behaviour (Rostad et al., 2019); others have found associations between only 'violent' pornography and some forms of non-consensual behaviour but not others (Ybarra & Thompson, 2018). Still other researchers have focused on intervening variables, including hostile masculinity and impersonal sex orientation, which has only resulted in less clarity in claims of association (Huntington et al., 2020; Kohut et al., 2021).

Reviewing these data we note that it remains the case that no simple conclusions can be drawn about associations between consuming (various kinds of) pornography and (various kinds of) (non-)consensual sexual behaviours. Despite this fact, many recent articles display an unwarranted confidence that the state of knowledge in regard to pornography consumption and consent is more settled than is in fact the case, with many making claims similar to Seabrook et al.: 'Previous research has documented connections between media use and violence against women' (Seabrook et al., 2019, p. 536; see also Palermo et al., 2019, p. 246; Rostad et al., 2019, p. 2137; Dawson et al., 2019, p. 588; Huntington et al., 2020, p. 3; de Heer et al., 2020, p. 2). Having read this book, the reader will understand that the actual data do not support such confident claims of a causal relationship (see Stanley et al., 2018, for a more nuanced account of the literature).

We note that the articles published since January 2018 also tend to continue to take a normative approach towards sex by, for example, referring to casual sex as being 'promiscuous' (quoted in Kohut et al., 2021, p. 648). Researchers continue to conflate consensual BDSM with violence in accounts of 'violent pornography' (Stanley et al., 2018; Ybarra & Thompson, 2018; Palermo et al., 2019; Rostad et al., 2019). We also note that articles continue to imply causality in their use of language and framing of questions – talking about, for example, 'the relationship between pornography consumption and sexually aggressive behavior' rather than 'the relationship between sexually aggressive behaviour and pornography consumption' (de Heer et al., 2020; see also Palermo et al., 2019; Rostad et al., 2019). We note that all of the articles we found on pornography use and consent used research methods from social psychology. We found no articles that attempted to measure consumers' understandings of consent, or which listened to their perspectives on how to make ethical decisions about consensual behaviour. This is important given the precise wording of the domain of healthy sexual development, which involves the individual learning to:

> Understand the nature and complexity of consent—not just their own but also other people's—in sexuality. They need to learn about the ethics of human relationships and how to treat other people ethically.
>
> (McKee et al., 2010, p. 17)

As we noted in Chapter 4, ethical and consensual conduct is contextual; it doesn't just mean ticking a box. There is a significant difference between being able to explain the thinking behind our ethical conduct towards people and just answering 'No' to a question about whether we would rape someone if we could get away with it.

Sexual learning and pornography consumption

We reviewed articles about sexual learning and pornography that were published after our systematic review – we note that we still cannot find research that seeks to answer the question: do people who consume pornography have better knowledge about how to have sex than people who do not?

We did find some articles about pornography and sex education more broadly. While all of the recent articles about consent we reviewed used methods derived from social psychology, several of the articles about the potential for pornography to function as sex education took qualitative approaches and were often published in journals with a more humanities focus. For example, Carboni and Bhana found that teenage girls used sexually explicit material to 'expand their knowledge' (Carboni & Bhana, 2019, p. 371); Chesser et al.

found that women used SEM to 'strengthen sexual subjectivity' (Chesser et al., 2018, p. 1234); and Fox and Bale found that 'media and pornography contribute affects that open up new possibilities for young people's emergent sexualities', offering sources of information as well as opportunities for pleasure (Fox & Bale, 2018, p. 405). Researchers still make the point that formal sex education is failing to provide young people with information about 'female sexual agency' (Carboni & Bhana, 2019, p. 386), sexual pleasure or desire (Carboni & Bhana, 2019, p. 386) or information about diverse sexual identities (Dawson et al., 2019). We again note that research with women allows for the possibility of positive education from engagement with sexually explicit materials for developing sexual agency and exploring sexual pleasure (Chesser et al., 2018; Carboni & Bhana, 2019) – but that we still did not find any research that posited the same possibility for heterosexual men.

By contrast to this work from the humanities perspective, the recent research we found in this area that used social psychological approaches often presented sexual learning as a negative thing. This was presented as negative in relation to 'risky sexual behaviors' (Shallo & Mengesha, 2018, p. 461), the risk of learning to have condomless sex (Wright et al., 2020, p. 1576) or the 'acceptance of teen sex' (Wright et al., 2018).

In raising concerns about what is learned from pornography, authors offered varied language that often moved away from discussing 'learning', 'education' and 'pedagogy'. While these were certainly used by social scientists (see, for example, Wright, Sun & Miezan, 2019) some authors referred instead to the 'influence' of pornography (Nelson et al., 2019) – a rough synonym for 'education', but one that denies the agency of learners. Shallo and Mengesha (2018) report on how undergraduate students in their research 'search' for SEM (suggesting greater agency of users); they also describe this as 'exposure' – again, suggesting that young people are victims of pornography, rather than willingly accessing it as a source of learning and pleasure.

Not all articles that take a quantitative approach present education as negative. A number of quantitative articles report on correlations between learning from pornography and other variables (Miller et al., 2018; Dawson et al., 2019; Charest & Kleinplatz, 2021; Rothman et al., 2021). However, none attempted to measure levels of knowledge about how to have sex. We still find ourselves with no data about whether people who consume pornography have more information about how to have (good) sex.

Porn literacy and pornography consumption

Our key question in regard to porn literacy is: do people who consume more pornography have a better understanding of how pornography works as a genre? It was encouraging that we found little new research continuing with the problematic idea that porn literacy simply means convincing young people that pornography is not 'realistic' (see Chapter 5) in order to prevent the transmission of bad messages – like having sex without condoms (Wright et al., 2021). Instead, we found that the last few years have produced some valuable research that gathers data from consumers about how they understand their porn consumption in order to develop an empirically based model of porn literacy – which is substantially more complex than understanding pornography as 'unrealistic'. For example, Attwood et al. (2018) found that consumers use pornography for a range of different reasons, from masturbation to education to exploration of identities or fantasies. This demands that we rethink porn literacy in terms of understanding the different kinds of pornography available, the uses to which they might be put and the ability of consumers to navigate these possibilities through their 'reading' of pornography. These authors reported that the consumers they talked to had never 'stumbled across' pornography, and were able to outline their search strategies, and why they looked for the particular kinds of material that they did: 'the acquisition of skills and the becoming practiced enough to view oneself as a hobbyist with tastes and preferences' (Attwood et al., 2018, p. 3747). Their data suggest that consuming more pornography leads to greater levels of porn literacy, though they do not explicitly measure this:

> Tastes in porn shift and develop with experience and knowledge, as with other kinds of cultural practices. In this extract, porn begins as unknown and monolithic – an 'it' – but becomes 'kinds' over time and with the investment of browsing.
>
> (Attwood et al., 2018, p. 3749; see also Goldstein, 2021, pp. 6, 8, 9, 15; Wright & Štulhofer, 2019, p. 43)

Other recent research reiterates that young people are aware of, and quite capable of replicating for researchers, cultural discourses about the harms of pornography. Researchers report on the 'third person' effect in which research participants believe that pornography does not harm them personally but may harm other people (Healy-Cullen et al., 2021), and therefore support 'education' programmes to teach the difference between 'pornography and sex in "real life"' (Lim et al., 2020, p. 2) (as discussed in Chapter 6).

Several recent articles report on the development of educational materials to teach porn literacy. While some retain a 'critical' approach that is not student-centred and assumes primarily negative effects from the consumption of pornography (Rothman et al., 2020), a more encouraging development has been the emergence of co-design with young people to develop programmes in porn literacy (Davis et al., 2020; Dawson et al., 2020). The programmes emerging from such approaches take a different approach to 'porn literacy', including the ability to 'communicate [their sexual] needs' (Davis et al., 2020, p. 8) and 'reducing shame regarding pornography' (Dawson et al., 2020, p. 1; see also Goldstein, 2020, p. 64).

Porn consumption and pleasure

Our review of recent articles on the relationship between consumption of pornography and sexual pleasure suggests that researchers have continued to focus on relationship satisfaction rather than pleasure *per se*. Some recent studies we reviewed about associations between pornography consumption and relationship satisfaction offer contradictory findings (Dwulit & Rzymski, 2019; Miller et al., 2019; Shuler et al., 2021), while others introduce intervening variables including masturbation (Perry, 2020) and moral disapproval of pornography (Guidry et al., 2020).

In addition to this ongoing work, however, it is reassuring to find that recent research has also begun to focus on pleasure as an important associate of pornography. A recent spate of qualitative research on women's pornography consumption and pleasure consistently reports on women's ambivalence about pornography consumption, with some aspects of pornography enhancing sexual pleasure, while others interfere with pleasure (Chadwick et al., 2018; Ashton et al., 2019; Carboni & Bhana, 2019; Marques, 2019). Common discomforts relate to concerns about sexism (Carboni & Bhana, 2019), misrepresentations of bodies, sexual acts and pleasure and 'concern for actors' wellbeing' (Ashton et al., 2019, p. 409). Marques gathered data using focus groups and interviews and found that women actively navigate gendered norms in order to gain sexual pleasure from pornography (Marques, 2019). Once again, we note that we have found no data on whether pornography use helps heterosexual men explore and embrace sexual pleasure, and that this work is qualitative in nature and so can offer no quantitative insights.

The closest we have found to research attempting to quantitatively measure the relationship between pornography consumption and levels of sexual pleasure is recent work that focuses on 'sexual satisfaction' or 'sexual wellbeing' – which is, at least, closer to sexual pleasure than is 'relationship satisfaction'. Studies in this area are currently contradictory (Wright, Sun, Steffen et al., 2019; Milas et al., 2020). However, they are beginning to explore a range of possible intervening variables, including religiosity (Perry & Whitehead, 2019), whether couples are in monogamous, consensually non-monogamous or non-consensually non-monogamous relationships (Rodrigues et al., 2021), how often pornography is used (Wright, Miezan, et al., 2018), whether pornography use is individual or partnered (Willoughby & Leonhardt, 2020; Bőthe et al., 2021).

As a final point we note that it is interesting that much of this recent crop of articles includes sexual pleasure but does not focus on it exclusively; it is only one part of a suite of indicators which usually includes some measure of relationship satisfaction. This could be interpreted either as a pleasingly holistic approach, or a continued insistence that sex should not be only about pleasure.

Unsystematic review: addiction

One recent trend in pornography research has been an increasing focus on pornography addiction. This may seem to be an elephant in the room – why are only mentioning this now, at the very end of the book?

We did not explore the question of addiction in our systematic reviews for two reasons. Firstly, it is not a domain of healthy sexual development – one can consume a lot of pornography and still have a healthy sex life. Secondly, we see this is a classic example of pornography research missing the point about healthy sexual development. Clearly being addicted to pornography – or sex, or masturbation – is not healthy. However, it is not clear that behaviours that are currently described as sex addiction (or pornography addiction) are actual health issues. Humanities researchers insist that these are moral issues; and some data from the social sciences support this contention.

Humanities researchers have written extensively about the expansion of the concept of addiction over the course of the 20th century to encompass behaviours as well as substances (Taylor, 2019). Often the term 'addiction' is used as a moral judgment (Clarkson & Kopaczewski, 2013) to keep people's behaviour 'within socially acceptable boundaries' (Keane, 2004). Importantly, researchers have noted that it is difficult to even generate a definition of 'addiction' to behaviours that does not include all leisure practices (Williams et al., 2020). To argue that a behaviour is addictive:

> simply due to increased dopaminergic activity and participants' feelings of short-term pleasure is simplistic and does not adequately differentiate—nor appreciate the complexity in attempting to differentiate—behavior that may be addictive from many forms of acceptable leisure behaviour.
>
> (Williams et al., 2020, p. 312)

Other researchers have argued that behaviours that are described as 'addictive' can equally well be understood as 'non-pathological evidence of learning' (Ley et al., 2014, p. 94). Indeed, some researchers go so far as to describe the concept of 'addiction' as 'a myth that provides a simple explanation of the outcomes of particular behaviours so that more thor-ough and ... complex explorations of the causes for those behaviors can be avoided' (Clarkson & Kopaczewski, 2013, p. 130).

Both humanities and social scientific researchers have critiqued models of sex and pornography addictions. Historians Reay, Attwood and Gooder, describe sex addiction as 'a response to cultural anxiety' (Reay et al., 2015, p. np), while Ley, Prause and Finn (as clinical psychologists and neurosci-entists) reject the concept of pornography addiction (Ley et al., 2014, p. 96). The American Psychiatric Association's *Diagnostic and Statistical Manual of Mental Disorders* has never recognised porn addiction (or, more broadly, sex addiction) as a phenomenon (American Psychiatric Association, 2013). Elsewhere, the argument that the release of chemicals such as dopamine into the brain is evidence of addiction has been described by neuroscientists as 'complete rubbish' (Herbert, cited in Clarkson & Kopaczewski, 2013, p. 132). Despite these rejections, Grubbs et al. highlight that

> The notion of problematic pornography use remains contentious in both academic and popular literature', with mental health experts being divided on the issue, and many pornography consumers who report their use of pornography as 'problematic'.
>
> (Grubbs et al., 2019, p. 397)

The fact that many people feel bad about their pornography use, and that they may self-identify as 'porn addicts', demands attention and explanation. But the model of porn addiction currently offered does not present a model of healthy use against which perceived addiction can be judged. Measures of porn addiction merely measure how ashamed respondents are of their current sexual practices, and an emerging literature on 'moral incongru-ence' and pornography addiction supports this point. Research has consist-ently shown that one of the most important variables in whether people feel they are addicted to pornography is how ashamed they are of pornography use – so-called 'moral incongruence' (Grubbs et al., 2015; Grubbs et al., 2018; Miller et al., 2018; Perry & Whitehead, 2019). We note that research-ers who take a normative view of sexuality have begun to challenge this finding (Palazzolo & Bettman, 2020) – but to do so they need to misrepre-sent the data published by Grubbs et al.

How, then, do we fit this tradition of pornography research into healthy sexual development? First, we note that the popularity of this form of research can be explained by forces outside of healthy sexual development. Ley et al. (2014) suggest that 'the tenacity and popularity of the porn addic-tion concept to describe high rates of [visual sexual stimuli] use appears to be driven by non-empirical forces' (Ley et al., 2014, p. 100). They propose that these include the dominance of moralistic discourses in societies with a strong religious orientation, and the profit motive of a 'lucrative, largely unregulated industry' (Ley et al., 2014, p. 98). In terms of our model of healthy sexual development, research on pornography addiction seems to consistently show that large numbers of people suffer shame about sexual pleasure. This data could potentially be used to understand the domain of healthy sexual development that requires that – in order to become happy, healthy sexual beings - we must embrace 'awareness and acceptance that sex can be pleasurable' (McKee et al., 2010, p. 17). From this perspective, the fact that a significant number of pornography users feel ashamed about their masturbatory practices demands that we start to explore how we could help lower their levels of sexual shame.

Limitations

Amongst the many issues that the social scientists in this team brought to the table was a clarity about the importance of the limitations of research projects – a modesty that is not always present in writing by humanities researchers. And so we note that in this project – as with every systematic review – it is possible that relevant articles have been omitted because they did not appear in the searches, despite the advice of the Delphi panel and the use of extensive databases for the searches. It is also possible that the search terms used were not entirely exhaustive. As always, there is a tension between the epistemic values of replicability and exhaustiveness (Fallis, 2008). Because this systematic review focused only on journal articles published in English within a specific timeframe (January 2000 to December 2017), books, book chapters, unpublished materials, material published not in English and material published before January 2000 and after December 2017 are by default excluded. In regard to the earlier date, it was intended that the cumulative nature of academic research should mean that the findings of earlier work would have informed the articles that were included; in regard to the later date, it was necessary to set a final date otherwise it would be impossible to finalise the analyses.

Future research

Another skill brought to the project by the social scientific members of the team was the idea that, at the end of reporting findings, suggestions should be made about directions for future research. This is less common in humanities writing. In this case, it is easy to say what we would like to see: pornography research that starts with an explicit definition of healthy sexual development, and that then explores the relationships between pornography and its audiences in relation to aspects of that definition of healthy sexuality. And we would like to see research that is not trapped in normative principles. We want to see research that understands that casual sex, masturbation and kink can be part of healthy sexual development – so long as they are consensual. We'd like to see research that is more open to engaging with a range of consumers, who are given space to share their experiences and engagements with pornography, and how this relates to healthy sexual development. This would mean that we, as researchers, invite pornography consumers to challenge us about the research questions, approaches and paradigms we use to understand pornography and its impacts, values and meanings. Importantly, we would also like to see less research on pornography that assumes causality where the evidence does not support such claims. This would lead to a reduced focus on 'effects' and 'impact' (unless there is evidence provided by researchers to support these claims).

Fifty years ago, the President's Commission on Obscenity and Pornography found that:

> there is a correlation between experience with erotic materials and general attitudes about sex: Those who have more tolerant or liberal sexual attitudes tend also to have greater experience with sexual material.
> (Commission on Obscenity and Pornography, 1970, p. 30)

As we noted, it also found that:

> Delinquent and nondelinquent youth generally report similar experiences with explicit sexual materials ... Available research indicates that sex offenders have had less adolescent experiences with erotica than other adult ... empirical research designed to clarify the question has found no evidence to date that exposure to explicit sexual materials plays a significant role in the causation of delinquent or criminal behaviour.
> (Commission on Obscenity and Pornography, 1970, pp. 30, 31, 32)

Academic research in the last 50 years has continued to find correlations between more 'tolerant' sexual attitudes (sometimes named 'permissive') and pornography use. The research has also continued, over and over, to try to prove that the Commission was wrong in finding no correlation between pornography and sexual violence, insisting that the finding of no correlation must be wrong and repeatedly seeking the elusive variable that will finally lock down a link. While this has not been achieved, discussions within and surrounding a continuing urge to find evidence of pornography's harms has pervaded public accounts of pornography and its claimed social and psychological effects. This demonstrates Law's (2004) argument that research methods often work as 'inscription devices', in that they can script and manifest certain ideals and realities about the objects we study and foreclose a range of other approaches or perspectives. Research methods (such as those used to measure pornography's effects) are iterative, in that they are repeated over time and through such repetition they come to be expected and regarded as being 'common sense'. As such, they make certain questions more urgent and expected (such as questions asked about pornography's effects over many decades), rendering other methods of inquiry more unlikely and more easily rejected. This is evident in questions commonly asked of pornography, such as a tendency to focus on 'relationship satisfaction' rather than sexual pleasure, a focus on sexual aggression ahead of discussing the minutiae of sexual consent and a focus on educating young people to reject pornography – for being a poor source of knowledge about sexual health, and for its 'unrealistic' depictions of sex – rather than exploring what young people seek, find, want and learn from pornography. In all such examples we note that attention to healthy sexual development is not the common focus in interdisciplinary research on pornography use; we think that it should be.

We hope that, after 50 years, we can now move to a different way of studying the relationships between pornography and its audiences. Let us explore the correlations between sexual pleasure and pornography consumption; pornography and lifelong learning about how to have sex; sexual agency and pornography consumption; pornography consumption and understandings and practice of consent– in short, between the consumption of pornography and healthy sexual development. It is an exciting prospect.

References

American Psychiatric Association. (2013). *Diagnostic and statistical manual of mental disorders (DSM-5®)*. American Psychiatric Publishing. http://ebookcentral.proquest.com/lib/uts/detail.action?docID=1811753

Ashton, S., McDonald, K., & Kirkman, M. (2019). Pornography and women's sexual pleasure: Accounts from young women in Australia. *Feminism and Psychology, 29*(3), 409–432. https://doi.org/10.1177/0959353519833410

Attwood, F., Smith, C., & Barker, M. (2018). 'I'm just curious and still exploring myself': Young people and pornography. *New Media and Society, 20*(10), 3738–3759. https://doi.org/10.1177/1461444818759271

Bőthe, B., Vaillancourt-Morel, M.-P., & Bergeron, S. (2021). Associations between pornography use frequency, pornography use motivations, and sexual wellbeing in couples. *Journal of Sex Research*, 1–15. https://doi.org/10.1080/00224499.2021.1893261

Carboni, N., & Bhana, D. (2019). Teenage girls negotiating femininity in the context of sexually explicit materials. *Sex Education*, *19*(4), 371–388. https://doi.org/10.1080/14681811.2019.1577730

Chadwick, S. B., Raisanen, J. C., Goldey, K. L., & van Anders, S. (2018). Strategizing to make pornography worthwhile: A qualitative exploration of women's agentic engagement with sexual media. *Archives of Sexual Behavior*, *47*(6), 1853–1868. https://doi.org/10.1007/s10508-018-1174-y

Charest, M., & Kleinplatz, P. J. (2021). What do young, Canadian, straight and LGBTQ men and women learn about sex and from whom? *Sexuality Research and Social Policy*. https://doi.org/10.1007/s13178-021-00578-7

Chesser, S., Parry, D., & Penny Light, T. (2018). Nurturing the erotic self: Benefits of women consuming sexually explicit materials. *Sexualities*, *22*(7–8), 1234–1252. https://doi.org/10.1177/1363460718791898

Clarkson, J., & Kopaczewski, S. (2013). Pornography addiction and the medicalization of free speech. *Jounal of Communication Inquiry*, *37*(2), 128–148. https://doi.org/10.1177/0196859913482330

Commission on Obscenity and Pornography. (1970). *The report of the commission on obscenity and pornography. Special introduction by Clive Barnes of the New York Times*. Bantam Books.

Davis, A. C., Wright, C. J. C., Murphy, S., Dietze, P., Temple-Smith, M. J., Hellard, M. E., & Lim, M. S. C. (2020). A digital pornography literacy resource co-designed with vulnerable young people: Development of "the gist". *Journal of Medical Internet Research*, *22*(6), e15964. https://doi.org/10.2196/15964

Dawson, K., Nic Gabhainn, S., & MacNeela, P. (2019). Dissatisfaction with school sex education is not associated with using pornography for sexual information. *Porn Studies*, *6*(2), 245–257. https://doi.org/10.1080/23268743.2018.1525307

Dawson, K., Nic Gabhainn, S., & MacNeela, P. (2020). Toward a model of porn literacy: Core concepts, rationales, and approaches. *Journal of Sex Research*, *57*(1), 1–15. https://doi.org/10.1080/00224499.2018.1556238

Dawson, K., Tafro, A., & Štulhofer, A. (2019). Adolescent sexual aggressiveness and pornography use: A longitudinal assessment. *Aggressive Behavior*, *45*(6), 587–597. https://doi.org/10.1002/ab.21854

de Heer, B. A., Prior, S., & Hoegh, G. (2020). Pornography, masculinity, and sexual aggression on college campuses. *Journal of Interpersonal Violence*, *36*(23–24), NP13582–NP13605. https://doi.org/10.1177/0886260520906186

Dwulit, A. D., & Rzymski, P. (2019). Prevalence, patterns and self-perceived effects of pornography consumption in polish university students: A cross-sectional study. *International Journal of Environmental Research and Public Health*, *16*(10), 1861. https://doi.org/10.3390/ijerph16101861

Fallis, D. (2008). Towards an epistomology of Wikipedia. *Journal of the American Society for Information Science and Technology*, *59*(10), 1662–1674.

Fox, N. J., & Bale, C. (2018). Bodies, pornography and the circumscription of sexuality: A new materialist study of young people's sexual practices. *Sexualities*, *21*(3), 393–409. https://doi.org/10.1177/1363460717699769

Goldstein, A. (2020). Beyond porn literacy: Drawing on young people's pornography narratives to expand sex education pedagogies. *Sex Education, 20*(1), 59–74. https://doi.org/10.1080/14681811.2019.1621826

Goldstein, A. (2021). Learner, laugher, lover, critic: Young women's normative and emerging orientations towards pornography. *Porn Studies, 8*(1), 5–20. https://doi.org/10.1080/23268743.2020.1736608

Grubbs, J. B., Exline, J. J., Pargament, K. I., Hook, J. N., & Carlisle, R. D. (2015). Trangression as addiction: Religiosity and moral disapproval as predictors of perceived addiction to pornography. *Archives of Sexual Behavior, 44*(1), 125–136. https://doi.org/10.1007/s10508-013-0257-z

Grubbs, J. B., Grant, J. T., & Engelman, J. (2018). Self-identification as a pornography addict: Examining the roles of pornography use, religiousness, and moral incongruence. *Sexual Addiction and Compulsivity, 25*(4), 269–292. https://doi.org/10.1080/10720162.2019.1565848

Grubbs, J. B., Perry, S. L., Wilt, J. A., & Reid, R. C. (2019). Pornography problems due to moral incongruence: An integrative model with a systematic review and meta-analysis. *Archives of Sexual Behavior, 48*(2), 397–415. https://doi.org/10.1007/s10508-018-1248-x

Guidry, R., Floyd, C. G., Volk, F., & Moen, C. E. (2020). The exacerbating impact of moral disapproval on the relationship between pornography use and depression, anxiety, and relationship satisfaction. *Journal of Sex and Marital Therapy, 46*(2), 103–121. https://doi.org/10.1080/0092623X.2019.1654579

Healy-Cullen, S., Taylor, J. E., Morison, T., & Ross, K. (2021). Using Q-methodology to explore stakeholder views about porn literacy education. *Sexuality Research and Social Policy.* https://doi.org/10.1007/s13178-021-00570-1

Huntington, C., Pearlman, D. N., & Orchowski, L. (2020). The confluence model of sexual aggression: An application with adolescent males. *Journal of Interpersonal Violence, 37*(1–2), 623–643. https://doi.org/10.1177/0886260520915550

Keane, H. (2004). Disorders of desire: Addiction and problems of intimacy. *Journal of Medical Humanities, 25*(3), 189–204.

Kohut, T., Landripet, I., & Štulhofer, A. (2021). Testing the confluence model of the association between pornography use and male sexual aggression: A longitudinal assessment in two independent adolescent samples from Croatia. *Archives of Sexual Behavior, 50*(2), 647–665. https://doi.org/10.1007/s10508-020-01824-6

Law, J. (2004). *After method: Mess in social science research.* Routledge.

Ley, D., Prause, N., & Finn, P. (2014). The emperor has no clothes: A review of the "pornography addiction" model. *Current Sexual Health Reports, 6*(2), 94–105. https://doi.org/10.1007/s11930-014-0016-8

Lim, M. S. C., Roode, K., Davis, A. C., & Wright, C. J. C. (2020). 'Censorship is cancer': Young people's support for pornography-related initiatives. *Sex Education, 21*(6), 660–673. https://doi.org/10.1080/14681811.2020.1845133

Maas, M. K., & Dewey, S. (2018). Internet pornography use among collegiate women: Gender attitudes, body monitoring, and sexual behavior. *SAGE Open, 8*(2), 2158244018786640. https://doi.org/10.1177/2158244018786640

Marques, O. (2019). Navigating, challenging, and contesting normative gendered discourses surrounding women's pornography use. *Journal of Gender Studies, 28*(5), 578–590. https://doi.org/10.1080/09589236.2019.1590184

McKee, A., Albury, K., Dunne, M., Grieshaber, S., Hartley, J., Lumby, C., & Mathews, B. (2010). Healthy sexual development: A multidisciplinary framework for research. *International Journal of Sexual Health, 22*(1), 14–19. https://doi.org/10.1080/19317610903393043

Milas, G., Wright, P., & Štulhofer, A. (2020). Longitudinal assessment of the association between pornography use and sexual satisfaction in adolescence. *Journal of Sex Research, 57*(1), 16–28. https://doi.org/10.1080/00224499.2019.1607817

Miller, D. J., Hald, G. M., & Kidd, G. (2018). Self-perceived effects of pornography consumption among heterosexual men. *Psychology of Men and Masculinity, 19*(3), 469–476. https://doi.org/10.1037/men0000112

Miller, D. J., McBain, K. A., Li, W. W., & Raggatt, P. T. F. (2019). Pornography, preference for porn-like sex, masturbation, and men's sexual and relationship satisfaction. *Personal Relationships, 26*(1), 93–113. https://doi.org/10.1111/pere.12267

Nelson, K. M., Perry, N. S., & Carey, M. P. (2019). Sexually explicit media use among 14–17-year-old sexual minority males in the U.S. *Archives of Sexual Behavior, 48*(8), 2345–2355. https://doi.org/10.1007/s10508-019-01501-3

Palazzolo, F., & Bettman, C. (2020). Exploring the lived experience of problematic users of internet pornography: A qualitative study. *Sexual Addiction and Compulsivity, 27*(1–2), 45–64. https://doi.org/10.1080/10720162.2020.1766610

Palermo, A. M., Dadgardoust, L., Caro Arroyave, S., Vettor, S., & Harkins, L. (2019). Examining the role of pornography and rape supportive cognitions in lone and multiple perpetrator rape proclivity. *Journal of Sexual Aggression, 25*(3), 244–257. https://doi.org/10.1080/13552600.2019.1618506

Perry, S. L. (2020). Is the link between pornography use and relational happiness really more about masturbation? Results from two national surveys. *Journal of Sex Research, 57*(1), 64–76. https://doi.org/10.1080/00224499.2018.1556772

Perry, S. L., & Whitehead, A. L. (2019). Only bad for believers? Religion, pornography use, and sexual satisfaction among American men. *Journal of Sex Research, 56*(1), 50–61. https://doi.org/10.1080/00224499.2017.1423017

Reay, B., Attwood, N., & Gooder, C. (2015). *Sex addiction: A critical history*. Polity.

Rodrigues, D. L., Lopes, D., Dawson, K., de Visser, R., & Štulhofer, A. (2021). With or without you: Associations between frequency of internet pornography use and sexual relationship outcomes for (non)consensual (non)monogamous individuals. *Archives of Sexual Behavior, 50*(4), 1491–1504. https://doi.org/10.1007/s10508-020-01782-z

Rostad, W. L., Gittins-Stone, D., Huntington, C., Rizzo, C. J., Pearlman, D., & Orchowski, L. (2019). The association between exposure to violent pornography and teen dating violence in grade 10 high school students. *Archives of Sexual Behavior, 48*(7), 2137–2147. https://doi.org/10.1007/s10508-019-1435-4

Rothman, E. F., Beckmeyer, J. J., Herbenick, D., Fu, T.-C., Dodge, B., & Fortenberry, J. D. (2021). The prevalence of using pornography for information about how to have sex: Findings from a nationally representative survey of U.S. adolescents and young adults. *Archives of Sexual Behavior, 50*(2), 629–646. https://doi.org /10.1007/s10508-020-01877-7

Rothman, E. F., Daley, N., & Alder, J. (2020). A pornography literacy program for adolescents. *American Journal of Public Health, 110*(2), 154–156. https://doi .org/AJPH.2019.305468

Seabrook, R. C., Ward, L. M., & Giaccardi, S. (2019). Less than human? Media use, objectification of women, and men's acceptance of sexual aggression. *Psychology of Violence, 9*(5), 536–545. https://doi.org/10.1037/vio0000198

Shallo, S. A., & Mengesha, W. W. (2018). Exposure to sexually explicit materials and its association with sexual behaviors of ambo university undergraduate students. *Ethiopian Journal of Health Sciences, 29*(4), 461–470. https://doi.org /10:4314/ejhs.v29i4.7. Corpus ID: 201615949.

Shuler, J., Brosi, M., Spencer, T., & Hubler, D. (2021). Pornography and romantic relationships: A qualitative examination of individual experiences. *Journal of Sex and Marital Therapy,* 1–16. https://doi.org/10.1080/0092623X.2021.1930308.

Stanley, N., Barter, C., Wood, M., Aghtaie, N., Larkins, C., Lanau, A., & Överlien, C. (2018). Pornography, sexual coercion and abuse and sexting in young people's intimate relationships: A European study. *Journal of Interpersonal Violence, 33*(19), 2919–2944. https://doi.org/10.1177/0886260516633204

Taylor, K. (2019). Pornography addiction: The fabrication of a transient sexual disease. *History of the Human Sciences, 32*(5), 56–83. https://doi.org/10.1177 /0952695119854624

Williams, D. J., Thomas, J. N., & Prior, E. E. (2020). Are sex and pornography addiction valid disorders? Adding a leisure science perspective to the sexological critique. *Leisure Sciences, 42*(3–4), 306–321. https://doi.org/10.1080/01490400 .2020.1712284

Willoughby, B. J., & Leonhardt, N. D. (2020). Behind closed doors: Individual and joint pornography use among romantic couples. *Journal of Sex Research, 57*(1), 77–91. https://doi.org/10.1080/00224499.2018.1541440

Wright, P. J., Herbenick, D., & Paul, B. (2020). Adolescent condom use, parent-adolescent sexual health communication, and pornography: Findings from a U.S. probability sample. *Health Communication, 35*(13), 1576–1582. https://doi.org /10.1080/10410236.2019.1652392

Wright, P. J., Herbenick, D., & Paul, B. (2021). Casual condomless sex, range of pornography exposure, and perceived pornography realism. *Communication Research.* https://doi.org/10.1177/00936502211003765

Wright, P. J., Miezan, E., & Sun, C. (2018). Pornography consumption and sexual satisfaction in a Korean sample. *Journal of Media Psychology, 31*(3), 164–169. https://doi.org/10.1027/1864-1105/a000246

Wright, P. J., & Štulhofer, A. (2019). Adolescent pornography use and the dynamics of perceived pornography realism: Does seeing more make it more realistic? *Computers in Human Behavior, 95,* 37–47. https://doi.org/10.1016/j.chb.2019 .01.024

Wright, P. J., Sun, C., & Miezan, E. (2019). Individual differences in women's pornography use, perceptions of pornography, and unprotected sex: Preliminary results from South Korea. *Personality and Individual Differences, 141*, 107–110. https://doi.org/10.1016/j.paid.2018.12.030

Wright, P. J., Sun, C., & Steffen, N. (2018). Pornography consumption, perceptions of pornography as sexual information, and condom use. *Journal of Sex and Marital Therapy, 44*(8), 800–805. https://doi.org/10.1080/0092623X.2018.1462278

Wright, P. J., Sun, C., Steffen, N. J., & Tokunaga, R. S. (2019). Associative pathways between pornography consumption and reduced sexual satisfaction. *Sexual and Relationship Therapy, 34*(4), 422–439. https://doi.org/10.1080/14681994.2017.1323076

Ybarra, M. L., & Thompson, R. E. (2018). Predicting the emergence of sexual violence in adolescence. *Prevention Science, 19*(4), 403–415. https://doi.org/10.1007/s11121-017-0810-4

Index